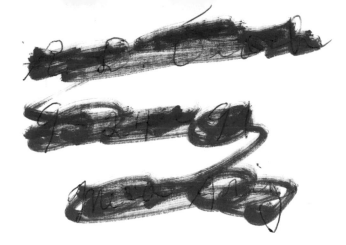

THE ILLUSTRATED HISTORY OF

TANKS

Andy Lightbody • Joe Poyer

PUBLICATIONS INTERNATIONAL, LTD.

Louis Weber, C.E.O.
Publications International, Ltd.
7373 North Cicero Avenue
Lincolnwood, Illinois 60646

Permission is never granted for commercial
purposes.

Manufactured in Yugoslavia.

h g f e d c b a

ISBN: 0-88176-651-8

Library of Congress Catalog Card Number: 89-
60928

Front cover: American M-48 Main Battle Tank **Back cover, clockwise from lower left:** American M-1 Abrams Main Battle Tank, American M-1 Abrams Main Battle Tank, American M-60 Main Battle Tank, American M-60 Main Battle Tank, American M-3 Medium Tank

Andy Lightbody is the Editorial Director for *International Defense & Aerospace Magazine* and is the Military/Aerospace Editor for CBS Radio. Mr. Lightbody's articles appear frequently in the national and military trade press.

Joe Poyer, noted military affairs journalist and novelist, contributes regularly to numerous military publications, including *International Defense Images* and *International Combat Arms*. Mr. Poyer is currently working with Andy Lightbody on a series of books, an *Encyclopedia of Terrorism*.

Contents

Right: American M-60 Main Battle Tank (left), American M-1 Abrams Main Battle Tank (right).

The Tank: History and Development

The Main Battle Tank

The first thing that strikes you when you climb down inside an M-1A1 Abrams tank is the smell of diesel fuel. It permeates everything. Next, you feel the chill; 63 tons of steel can hold a lot of cold.

Inside the massive turret three of the four-member crew sit. The commander has the right-hand seat below the largest hatch. He can stand with his head and shoulders out of the hatch or sit buckled into his seat and watch the outside world through six periscopes that give him 360° of vision.

To the commander's left, you eye the gunner's seat with its hooded night sight. Using the night sight, the gunner can "see" through darkness, fog, smoke, or dust almost as clearly as if it were full, clear daylight. You rest your hand on the breech of the M256 120 millimeter smoothbore gun filling the center of the turret and glance at the ammunition locker behind the loader's position on the left. Inside, rounds are nestled: tank-killing sabot rounds designated 827 (narrow diameter rods of depleted uranium, one of the hardest and densest materials known, surrounded by plastic sheaths that fit snugly into the gun's bore) or M830 HEAT (high-explosive, antitank) rounds.

The driver's seat, in the front center of the tank body proper, has a curious set of handlebars before it, and you realize that the driver steers the tank with them. On each end of the handlebars is a twist-type handgrip, exactly as on a motorcycle, that controls fuel feed. Above the driver's seat is a viewing hatch. When this is closed, the driver has a choice of three periscopes, including an image intensifier that replaces the center periscope for night driving if buttoned up. The driver's seat reclines because, with the hatch shut, there is no room to sit up.

As big as they are, tanks are still cramped on the inside. As you sit in the commander's seat, you wonder how four crewmembers can find room to sit, let alone ride and fight and often eat and sleep as well. Veteran tankers of World War II and the Korean War, however, would marvel at the amount of room inside the M-1A1 Abrams.

The tremendous weight of the M-1A1 tank (126,000 pounds), like any modern tank, is due primarily to its armor. Gone are the days when cast-steel plate provided protection against enemy antitank gunners. The M-1A1 is covered with Chobham-like armor, a sophisticated mix of steel, plastic, and ceramic plates. Production of a new type of armor combining depleted uranium and steel will soon begin. But you may wonder how well any armor will hold up when a Soviet T-80 125mm sabot round punches it at a velocity of 5,000+ feet per second.

Surprisingly, the tank is not as high as you might expect. From turret roof to the ground is only eight feet. You are impressed with every other aspect of the M-1A1's massiveness. It is 26 feet long and a little over 11 feet wide. Fully fueled and loaded for combat, it weighs 63 tons. But painted in three-color camouflage, it seems diminished when you walk a short distance away and view it against a line of trees. Then you remember that it is the most powerful land fighting vehicle in the world.

The Main Battle Tank (MBT), for brute power, is the most awesome fighting machine ever invented. The MBT exists for only one reason: to kill the enemy tanks so that infantry can occupy ground.

Critics complain that the tank has become too expensive, too heavy, too unwieldy, and too vulnerable to antitank weapons. History does not support this. Ever since Lieutenant Colonel Ernest D. Swinton climbed into the first Mark I tank on September 15, 1916, and kicked its engine to life, the tank's imminent demise has been reported. Tanks have fought in every major, and most minor, military engagements since 1916. They charged through German lines in 1918; they overran Poland, France, and most of European Russia in 1939–42; and they led the invasion into the German heartland from east and west in 1944–45. Tanks smashed the North Korean drive into South Korea in 1950, and the tank battles fought in the Sinai Desert in 1956, 1967, and 1973 have become legendary. While tanks played a minor role in the fighting in South Vietnam, the T-55 in the hands of North Vietnamese tankers spearheaded the 1975 offensive that broke the South Vietnamese Army. In 1982, Israeli tanks met and defeated the best of the Soviet tanks (T-62s and T-72s) in the hands of Syrian tankers. Massive tank battles, the largest and most deadly since Word War II, were fought along the Iraq–Iran border from 1980 to 1988. No, the modern tank is very much alive. It is still the first choice for knocking out the enemy and taking charge, and will be well into the next century.

What Is a Tank?

The basic definition of a "tank" is an armored vehicle moving on an endless track and armed with a large-caliber gun. Beyond that, a tank can be, and has been, just about anything its designers have wanted it to be. In this book, however, we will concentrate on tanks that are designed to punch through enemy lines so that following infantry can occupy ground. As we shall see, this is a definition that was not universally accepted even as late as 1946.

Armor—An Early History The concept of armored vehicles is not new. It probably occurred to whoever invented the chariot that if the sides were built-up a little higher and thicker, the driver

Right: The British Mark IV was a commonly used armored fighting vehicle on the western front in 1917 and early 1918. There were two versions: The male carried two six-pounder cannons; the female was armed with four machine guns. **Top left:** State-of-the-art tank design is represented by the American M-1 Abrams. **Top right:** The first tank to see actual combat was the British Mark I. It was 26 feet long, weighed 28 tons, and traveled at 4 mph. The trailing wheels helped turn the monster.

and the archer or spearman riding in it would be relatively safe from the arrows and spears of the enemy.

The horse soldier was the next step in development. As long as horses were the main source of locomotion, it was more efficient for one man to ride one horse than for one or more horses to pull one or more men in a wheeled wagon that continually needed repairs. The soldier on horseback had several advantages over the foot soldier: mobility, speed, and height. Armor was necessary for mounted soldiers to protect them from spears, slings, stones, swords, and arrows.

By the time Alexander the Great swept across the face of southern Europe and central Asia in the middle of the fourth century BC, armor for the mounted man had become a specialized item. Medieval European knights made the transition from Roman plate and strap armor to chain mail during the tenth and eleventh centuries. By the thirteenth century, when arrowheads capable of penetrating chain mail were universally adopted, armor makers switched back to plate. In the late fifteenth century, Leonardo da Vinci observed mounted knights and saw other applications for armor. He drew numerous designs for vehicles that were coated with metal armor and that carried bombs or fired a cannon. Armor, mobility, and fire power have ancient foundations.

From Muscle Power to Mechanical Power   The invention of firearms put armor makers out of business. It wasn't until the latter part of the nineteenth century, when the science of metallurgy caught up with the development of artillery and firearms, that armor once again became a viable concept. But the weight of the armor needed to stop projectiles moving at speeds of up to 1,800 feet per second was so great that muscle power was no longer sufficient to carry it.

In the 1850s the steam tractor was a brand new invention. A huge, snorting monster of iron and brass, it depended on a coal- or wood-fired boiler to produce steam to move a "walking beam" lever that in turn rotated large-diameter iron wheels. The steam tractor was beginning to drag plows and harvesters across the farmlands of Europe and America.

At the start of the Crimean War in 1853, dozens of plans to harness the power of steam tractors to haul ammunition, men, guns, and even trailers on which artillery pieces were mounted flooded the War Office in London. Most were summarily rejected. Steam tractors were ungainly monsters: They weighed tons and required vast amounts of fuel to keep them going as well as a small army of mechanics to tend them. Shipping space on sailing vessels was scarce, as was fuel in the areas of the Crimea occupied by the British.

The British Army did buy its first powered land vehicle the next year, the Boydell Traction Engine, but it was used to tow guns at the Woolwich Arsenal in London. The purchase was noteworthy because the Boydell Traction Engine was the first powered vehicle to be used by a military force for any purpose. The Boydell had a "footed wheel": Spokes extended from a hub and ended in large square pads or feet. As the wheel revolved, the "pads" walked.

During the American Civil War (1861–65), the rapid mobility made possible by railroads was studied most intensely by German staff officers, whose recommendations led to victory in the Franco–Prussian War in 1871.

The Confederate States of America are generally credited with deploying the first powered, armored, and armed military vehicle. Ross Winans built a steam tractor that was covered with armor and fitted with a cannon in 1861. It was driven to Harper's Ferry Arsenal in what was then Virginia—and promptly captured by Union troops. Proponents of armor learned a valuable lesson: As powerful as an armored and armed vehicle may seem, it must still be accompanied and protected by infantry.

The Boer War (1899–1902) saw the first practical use of armored vehicles. The British armored four Fowler B5 Traction engines with boilerplate and sent them to South Africa to tow guns and supply wagons. Special armored wagons holding 30 riflemen were also fitted up.

The Reciprocating Engine

In 1887 Gottlieb Daimler invented the reciprocating gasoline engine. Within a decade, engines with power-to-weight ratios that could move reasonably sized vehicles over long distances were available. Military designers did not waste any time in taking advantage of the gasoline engine.

In 1898 Fredrick Simms of England built a four-wheeled bicycle powered by a small gasoline engine, mounted with a Maxim machine gun, and protected by a steel plate attached to the handlebars. Two years later and across the Atlantic in the United States, Colonel R.P. Davidson refitted two Duryea motorcars to carry Colt machine guns. Each car was protected by a small area of armor on the front grille. But the honor of devising the first true armored vehicle belongs to the Russian inventor Divinski, who built a specially designed steam-powered vehicle in 1900. It was underpowered and never used, but it led to further studies and increased interest of the Russian army.

The pace now began to accelerate. In 1901 E.J. Pennington, an American designer, shielded a motorcar and mounted a Maxim

Far right: During the 1850s the British Army purchased a Boydell Traction Engine with "footed" wheels. **Top:** Leonardo da Vinci's "armored turtle" was to be powered by men turning cranks. Muskets furnished the firepower while pikes kept the enemy at bay. **Center:** Winans' steam battery, built in Baltimore in 1861. **Bottom:** Colonel R.P. Davidson designed and built a number of armored bicycle and automobile designs. He is shown here with two military students in a Duryea tri-car armed with a machine gun and protected by armor plate.

machine gun behind armor. In France the following year, armor and a Hotchkiss machine gun were mounted on a Panhard motor-car. It was used successfully in Morocco for patrol work. In Britain in 1902 Fred Simms built a "war car," the forerunner of the modern armored car. Simms' car was armor-plated and carried a small-caliber, quick-firing cannon.

In France in 1904 another partially armored car was designed. This time a machine gun was mounted on the roof. Two were built; one was bought by the Russians and the other by the French Army. That same year, the German Army purchased a Daimler motorcar fitted with a Maxim machine gun in a turret. In 1908 the firm of Armstrong-Whitworth designed and built an armored car powered by a 40 horsepower engine and armed with a Maxim machine gun.

During the next four years, an increasing number of armored car designs were built and tested by various armies. But the Italians in 1912 were the first to use one in combat—an Isotta-Fraschini car fitted with a turret and a machine gun—against the Turks in North Africa, in what is now Libya.

World War I

The start of World War I in August 1914 took everyone by surprise. A system of interlocking treaties designed to prevent war in fact caused a war that no one really wanted. Once started, it took on a life of its own. Trench warfare began within the first month and had become a "fact of the war" by the end of October and the First Battle of Ypres.

On the western front, German armies seeking passage into France marched swiftly into Belgium. The violation of Belgian neutrality left Britain no choice but to honor a treaty dating from the beginning of the previous century to protect Belgium—and by extension the British Isles. The British Expeditionary Force crossed the Channel and marched, with Belgian and French columns, to take up defensive positions. Cavalry swept ahead—into machine-gun fire. Infantry fared no better; rapid firing artillery and the machine gun drove them underground. The Germans, marching on Paris, encountered the same curtain of steel and lead at the Marne River and retreated to the Aisne River. There they stood. Slowly, the networks of opposing trenches grew in both directions until they writhed from the English Channel north of Dunkirk to the Swiss border.

In the east, hundreds of thousands of Russian troops marched from Russia and Poland toward East Prussia. German artillery and machine guns stopped them cold at Tannenberg and the Masurian Lakes and then slowly drove them back—into the trenches.

British Efforts Winston Churchill was First Lord of the Admiralty in Great Britain in the summer of 1914. A young and ambitious politician, he had already made his mark as a soldier and journalist. Churchill had served in a variety of government posts, including Home Secretary, and much of the progressive social legislation of pre-World War I Great Britain had been introduced by David Lloyd George and Churchill.

As First Lord, Churchill was perceptive enough to see that the international flap over the murder of Archduke Ferdinand (the act that ostensibly triggered the war) and the subsequent demands for mobilization were not going to go away. Churchill closely watched the progress of mobilization in Serbia, Austria, and Russia and realized that soon Germany would be dragged in by its treaty commitments. If Germany came in, France, bound by its treaty commitments, would march. If France marched, then Britain would have no choice but to declare war. During the last two weeks of July 1914, Churchill gave orders that positioned the British fleet to best advantage, and in the opening days of the war, the threat of the German battle fleet was contained.

This successful denial of the high seas to the German fleet, plus his experience as a frontline soldier in India and Africa, gave Churchill added stature in the war planning councils of the British government in the early days of the war. He clamored early and loudly for mechanical means to safely move infantry across bullet- and shrapnel-swept battlefields. In Belgium, he quickly ordered Royal Navy Air Service personnel, charged with defending Antwerp and British airfields against the approaching German juggernaut, to use Rolls Royce armored cars. These worked well on roads but were of little use in the no-man's-land that developed between the opposing trench systems. Artillery, acting like a million plows, churned the area into a morass of shell craters that wheeled vehicles could not traverse. The least hint of rain created a sea of mud that bogged down men, horses, and vehicles. Something better than wheels was needed to traverse this wasteland.

It was not until 1903, nearly a century after the invention of the endless track, that Benjamin Holt, an American, designed and built the "caterpillar," a workable, durable endless track. Basically, the caterpillar track is a system of flat steel plates hinged together to form a loop. Drive wheels at the front and back shape the track into an oblong. As the drive wheels turn, they ratchet the track ahead one plate at a time, providing the vehicle with its own road. Holt intended his invention for farming tractors, but he and others were quick to realize the track's potential in warfare.

French artillery Captain la Vavasseur submitted a caterpillar design in 1905 for a gun-carrying vehicle. Gunther Burstyn sub-

Right: The armored car's cross-country ability was limited by its need for roads. The caterpillarlike tractor tread was the solution. Benjamin Holt invented the caterpillar tread for his agricultural tractor. **Far right, above:** Fredrick Simms designed and built this armored car in 1902. **Far right, below:** The first successful armored vehicle to see combat was the Italian Isotta-Fraschini. It had a machine gun in a revolving turret. The Isotta-Fraschini was the basic design for armored cars until opening stages of WW II.

11

mitted a similar design based on Holt's traction method in 1911. L. de Mole, an Australian designer, tried twice, in 1911 and 1915, to interest the British War Office in his caterpillar-tracked designs; he even built working models. But as late as 1915 the answer was the same from every war office to every inventor: no interest.

Churchill, frustrated in his efforts to have the Army consider an armored "land cruiser," found funds in the Admiralty budget for their development. After several false starts, including a wheeled shield that proved too heavy, the use of an endless track driven by a gasoline engine was proposed. A competing idea was a tricycle-type motor vehicle based on the Daimler-Foster artillery tractor that would carry three sets of twin four-inch naval guns mounted on 45-foot-diameter wheels; not surprisingly, the vehicle was nicknamed "Big Wheel." The wheel diameter was necessary to attain the arc needed to cross a nine-foot-wide trench, a distance specified by the War Department.

Churchill was intrigued by both ideas. In February 1915 he set up an organization, operating under the name of Landships Committee, to study and recommend the best design for a landship. The two initial designs soon proved impractical, but work went on.

Colonel E. D. Swinton was an officer on the staff at British Expeditionary Forces Headquarters in France. In late 1914, he suggested that the Holt agricultural caterpillar tractor be used to build an armored infantry carrier. The idea was considered by the Committee on Imperial Defense in November of that year and dropped after a brief, unrealistic test, although Churchill pushed hard for its adoption.

Meanwhile, the Landships Committee had fastened onto the idea of the caterpillar tread. Two naval officers were sent to the United States to procure examples. They returned with two farming vehicles, a Killen-Strait tractor, which had wooden tracks covered with steel sheets, and a Bullock Creeping Grip tractor.

In mid-1915 a famous British engineer, Sir William Tritton, joined the Landships Committee. Tritton worked with Major W.G. Wilson to build a steel box on 12-foot-long treads. To help steer the contraption, two large wheels were attached to an outrigger at the back. A rotating turret holding a two-pounder gun was designed for the vehicle but never fitted. Nicknamed "Little Willie" after the German Kaiser, it passed every test except crossing the nine-foot trench.

Tritton and Wilson found a solution to crossing the trench that was to point tank design in the right direction for all time. They found their answer in Commander Hetherinton's Big Wheel. Tritton and Wilson reasoned that only the lower arc of a wheel was in contact with the ground at any one point in time. If they formed the caterpillar tread into a rhomboid shape the bottom of which was the same length and shape as the arc of the 45-foot wheel, then it should traverse a nine-foot-wide trench. A new vehicle based on this principle was quickly designed and built. Tritton and Wilson also slung the armored body between the tracks to lower its center of gravity.

Nicknamed "Big Willy," the vehicle was demonstrated to the War Office in January 1916 and was well received. In February 1916, 100 landships were ordered. Because the well-known author H.G. Wells had described "landships" in his novels, the term landship was deemed too descriptive. For security reasons, the contract referred to the land cruisers as water tanks. Instantly, the term was shortened to "tank."

French Efforts The British kept the development of their tanks so secret that not even the French had an inkling of their work. Through early work on armored cars, the French Ministry of War was oriented to the use of armored vehicles. At least 136 armored cars were ordered in August 1914.

The impetus in France to use tanks originally came from the Schneider factory, which specialized in armaments. Impressed by the usefulness of armored cars, Schneider's engineers began to search for a vehicle capable of operating in no-man's-land. A Schneider engineer saw a Holt caterpillar tractor while visiting England in January 1915. The Schneider Company bought two tractors and throughout the spring and summer of 1915 used them as the basis for developing a "cross-country armored vehicle."

At the beginning of December 1915, a respected French artillery officer, Colonel J.B.E. Estienne, submitted a plan to the Minister of War for an armed and armored fighting vehicle. He was put in touch with the engineers at Schneider, and by the end of the month a comprehensive plan for a tracked, armed, and armored vehicle was complete. Testing was successfully conducted during January 1916, and 400 vehicles were ordered from Schneider on February 26, 1916—less than two weeks after the British had ordered production of their tank.

Tanks into Battle In Britain, Big Willy had been refined into the Mark I tank. The Mark I was 26 feet long, weighed 28 tons, could move at four miles per hour, and had a range of 15 miles. A crew of eight was required to steer, operate the two engines and transmissions, and load and fire the guns. Two large wheels were attached at the rear to help steer when making wide turns. The Mark I was built in "male" and "female" versions. The male carried two naval six-pounder (57mm) guns mounted in sponsons on either side because a turret would have made the tank top-

Top: Little Willie was the first armored vehicle to be successfully mated with caterpillar-type treads. It was little more than an armored box mounted above modified caterpillar-style treads. Trials proved the value of the tread, although tread length was insufficient to cross a trench. **Bottom:** Little Willie was redesigned. The tread was lengthened and the vehicle's center of gravity lowered. The result was "Big Willie," shown here. Testing was completed by January 1916.

heavy. The female version was armed with four Vickers .303 machine guns. By 1918 the British had developed eight variations of the original Mark I tank, Marks I through VIII.

The Mark I carried 0.39 inch of armor, which protected it from rifle and machine-gun fire but not cannon or the 13.5mm Mauser antitank rifle the Germans quickly issued. Tactics were developed by Colonel J. C. Fuller that called for the tanks to be used en masse ahead of large cavalry and infantry forces.

In August 1916, 60 tanks and crews arrived in France. Sir Douglas Haig's offensive on the Somme was bogging down while casualties mounted into the tens of thousands. Despite pressure from London not to do so, Haig resolved to use the tanks to shore up, rather than lead, his infantry.

On September 15, 1916, tanks attacked for the first time ever. They beat their way across the soggy, churned-up land between the Somme and Ancre rivers and into disaster. Of 49 tanks leaving their assembly point, only 32 arrived at the start positions. Only nine tanks made it across no-man's-land; the rest either broke down or were bogged down. The tank attack served only to reveal the new weapon to the Germans.

Tanks were not used again until the Battle of Arras in April 1917. Two new models, the Mark II and Mark III, had strengthened armor, but they were still terribly vulnerable to armor-piercing bullets, which did great damage to vehicles and crews. The stronger, better armored, and more heavily gunned Mark IV tank was used in the Ypres Offensive. But the Mark IVs became mired in mud, turning them into objects of ridicule on both sides.

Cambrai, however, proved to be the turning point. At Cambrai, for the first time, the tankers were allowed to use their tanks as they should have been used from the beginning. Four hundred tanks were secretly massed behind British lines. No preliminary artillery bombardment was permitted, thus the farmland separating the two forces was not churned into a muddy bog. As each tank moved out at dawn on November 20, 1917, it carried a huge bundle of branches.

The Mark IV tanks were divided into companies of 12 and moved in triangular formations of threes. Each company was followed by infantrymen 100 yards behind. German troops were astonished to see camouflage-painted monsters looming out of the dawn mist. They ran as the tanks smashed the barbed wire under their treads and rolled to the edge of the trenches. The bundles of wood were tipped into the trenches, and the tanks rumbled across.

British tanks led an advance of six miles that day along a front seven miles wide. There were 7,000 British casualties—only a

tenth of the casualties on the first day of the Somme. But the British tanks were too slow to exploit their gains. They were unable to penetrate to the rear of the German line, and proper coordination had not been arranged with the infantry. Full realization of their potential would have to await a future war, but the lessons were there for those perceptive enough to see them.

The French, meanwhile, had developed three types of tanks, or *chars d' assaut*. The first, the Schneider, was 20 feet long, had a 60 horsepower engine, and was armed with a short-barrel 75mm gun and two Hotchkiss machine guns. The second was the Saint-Chamond. It was 26 feet long, had an 80 horsepower engine, and carried a long-barrel 75mm field gun and four Hotchkiss machine guns. Both were little more than armored boxes mounted atop the Holt tractor chassis. The third was a light tank, the Renault FT-17. It was 13 feet long and was powered by a 35 horsepower engine. One version mounted a 37mm gun; the other was armed only with a Hotchkiss machine gun.

French *chars* were first used in April 1917 along the Aisne River. Tactically, the French divided their tanks into *gruppes* of 16 each with a Renault FT-17 to serve as a command tank. But the French made the same mistake the British had and fed their tanks piecemeal into battle to support infantry.

In February 1917 revolution blazed across Russia. By November, the Bolsheviks had deposed the Kerensky government. An armistice was signed at Brest-Litvosk, and Germany rushed troops from the eastern to the western front in a desperate bid to mount a spring offensive before the Americans arrived in force. The German spring offensive drove 38 miles toward Paris.

On July 18, 1918, the French 10th Army hurled itself at the German Army at Soissons in a counterattack that opened the Second Battle of the Marne. French General Charles Mangin ordered the attack to begin with no artillery bombardment. Several hundred tanks loomed out of the morning mist to take the Germans by surprise. The result was 30,000 prisoners, 800 captured field guns, and the end of the German offensive. From this point on, the tank would be considered indispensable on the battlefield.

Until Cambrai, the Germans had dismissed the tank as little more than a terror weapon. After Cambrai, they changed their minds, but too late. Although the Germans used some 200 tanks before the war ended, most were captured British or French vehicles. The Germans designed and built only 20 A-7Vs, a heavy tank of 32 tons armed with a 57mm gun and six Maxims. The A-7V required a crew of 18.

The United States had no tanks of its own when troops arrived in France. French Renaults, British Mark Vs, and later versions were

14

Clockwise from top left: The trench proved the undoing of many early tanks; the Schneider tank was the first operational French battlefield tank; combat experience taught tankers the value of carrying bundles of twigs that could be dropped into enemy trenches to make them easier to cross; the Renault FT-17 saw wide use during WW I by French, American, and Italian tankers; Mark IV tanks were largely useless throughout 1917 because of muddy conditions.

borrowed. George Patton, Jr., then a colonel, earned a Distinguished Service Cross during the Meuse-Argonne battle when he gathered tank crews whose Renaults had been knocked out by German 77mm cannons and attacked German machine-gun positions.

Italy built 100 Fiat 3000 light tanks, a close copy of the French Renault. The Italian Army confined its use of tanks to the infantry support role.

The Allies quickly realized that building tanks to varying designs was inefficient. Production chores were divided up, and the Mark VIII was being assembled in France with British-produced armor and American-built engines when Germany surrendered.

The Tank Between Wars

The key to understanding the tank's development between 1920 and 1939 lies in the way each nation's military planners viewed these armored monsters. The French were convinced that future wars would be static, as the 1914–18 conflict had been, and that artillery and the machine gun would rule supreme. This led them to see the tank as a mobile machine gun or artillery piece to assist infantry in attacking prepared defensive positions.

Great Britain In Britain, the development of tank tactics after the war diverged sharply from the experience gained at Cambrai and Amiens. The British developed two types of infantry in reaction to static trench warfare. The first type was to be highly mobile and trained to exploit breakthroughs. The other type was to gain those breakthroughs by plodding forward with empty rifle chambers and fixed bayonets, exactly as they had done since 1915.

Tanks were designed to complement these infantry roles. A light reconnaissance tank was to range behind enemy lines to gather information, exactly as cavalry had done in an earlier day. A heavy, or infantry, tank, moving at the walking speed of a man, was to clear a way through enemy machine-gun nests, barbed wire, and trenches. A combination light-to-medium tank—termed a cruiser—was to engage other tanks as close to their home ground as possible and then exploit the breakthroughs made by the heavy tanks and infantry.

Charles de Gaulle, a veteran of World War I and a teacher of military history at Saint Cyr, France's equivalent to West Point, and Briton B.H. Liddell Hart, also a veteran of World War I and a military instructor and author, protested what they saw as the improper use of the tank. De Gaulle in *The Army of the Future* (1934) and Liddell Hart in *The Defense of Britain* (1939) wrote that the proper use of armor was to achieve breakthroughs that

mechanized infantry could then exploit. They both insisted the tank should be heavily gunned and armored to defeat the enemy's tanks, which would surely be trying to stop them. Both men were ignored by their respective military establishments.

Liddell Hart protested that rigid categorization limited a tank's overall effectiveness. The reconnaissance tank, with its light armor, was vulnerable to anything above small arms fire, effectively becoming a mobile coffin. Cruiser tanks were underpowered and under-gunned and thus could not range against more heavily armed enemy tanks. Infantry tanks were so badly under-gunned and slow that they became sitting ducks for antitank weapons or more powerfully armed tanks.

Despite these protests and the experiences of World War I, the concepts of armored divisions designed for "exploitation" and tank brigades to support infantry divisions became operational in the British Army—and stayed so until 1946.

The Soviet Union and Germany The Soviet Union came late to the tank. The Imperial Russian government lacked the resources to develop the armored car further. When Bolshevik forces in 1919 captured two Renault tanks supplied by France to White Russian forces, their interest was excited. So excited that by 1936 and the start of the Spanish Civil War, the Soviets had built 21,000 tanks.

Germany was forbidden to develop tanks by the Treaty of Versailles. Their army was also strictly limited. During the 1920s and early 1930s, the German Army maintained secret relations with the Soviet Army. German weaponry was tested and tactics practiced in secret locations within the Soviet Union. By 1932 the Soviets had absorbed sufficient German tactical thinking that they had established a mechanized corps of tanks and infantry. But Stalin's purges between 1935 and 1939 eliminated most of the Russian Army's experienced ranking armor officers. They were replaced with young, inexperienced commanders in all branches, and Soviet tank tactics gravitated toward the British and French two-pronged approach of supporting infantry with one type of tank and achieving breakthroughs with another.

The German Army's lack of experience with tanks by 1918 had left them with few preconceived notions about tank warfare. The Treaty of Versailles may have forbidden tanks, but the German officer corps, as determined to avenge German honor as the French had been after 1871, pursued the idea of armored warfare assiduously. When Hitler came to power in 1933 and authorized rearmament in defiance of the Versailles Treaty, priority was given to the development of armor. The Nazi government, which assisted General Francisco Franco's fascist forces during the Spanish Civil War, used that war as a "testing ground" for

The Tank

Basically, a tank is an armored box that is armed with a gun and moves on endless treads. But such a simple description begs a host of details. It is probably fair to say that the tank is one of the most complex ground vehicles ever developed.

Suspension The tank chassis carries the entire weight of the vehicle—63 tons in the case of the M-1A1 Abrams. A suspension system to absorb road and off-road shocks for a tracked vehicle is more complicated than for a wheeled vehicle because there are more points in contact with the ground. Independent suspension systems have proved most effective. Torsion bars—steel rods that flex and twist—are used to absorb shock. In modern tanks they are mounted transversely between the treads. In the M-1 Abrams Main Battle Tank, the

rear wheels, which are really drive sprockets, lever the tread of linked steel plates forward in a continuous loop. The tread is suspended between the drive sprocket and the idler—the wheel at the front—and guided across the top by rollers. The tread is held in contact with the ground by additional larger rollers called road wheels. The driving wheels can also be placed at the front and the idler at the rear, as was the case with the M-4 Sherman.

Engines Tank engines are characterized by high power-to-weight ratios that provide the tank commander with a reserve of power for difficult mobility—crossing ditches or antitank barriers or maneuvering during battle. The ideal tank engine accelerates quickly, is air cooled, burns a fuel with a low ignition point, requires little periodic maintenance, and is very reliable. Until

recently, the diesel was considered to be the ideal tank engine. It met all of the qualifications above to one degree or another and was superior to the gasoline engine because its fuel was not nearly as volatile.

The latest MBT designs, the American M-1A1 Abrams and the Soviet T-80, are powered by a gas turbine engine, which is a small jet engine developed from the engines that power aircraft and naval vessels. The gas turbine is smaller and more compact than the diesel; it burns a wider variety of fuels; and it has a higher power-to-weight output. Fuel for gas turbine engines is more volatile than diesel fuel, but appropriate safety measures—all fuel tanks located outside the sealed crew and ammunition compartments—have been taken to minimize this danger. The Israeli Merkava II and III MBTs continue to

use diesel engines, but it is not improbable that they will be reconfigured with gas turbine engines in the near future. Engines are usually mounted at the rear, except in the Merkava, where it is mounted at the front to serve as additional armor for the crew.

Turret The tank's turret is a gun mount similar to that found on a naval ship. The tank's main gun is mounted inside the turret, which must be large enough to allow room for the gun to recoil, as well as hold the gunner, the tank commander, and the loader, who must have room to stand to heft shells into the gun's breech. In some designs, like the Swedish Stridsvagn 103B and the Soviet T-64/T-72/T-80 series, the loader is replaced by an automatic feed mechanism that permits a lower turret design.

Vision In combat, the tank is "buttoned up." This means all

hatches closed, all crewmembers in their interior compartments, and the entire tank sealed against entry of nuclear, biological, or chemical war agents. The crew "sees" with periscopes that provide 360° of vision and thermal sights that allow them to see through fog, darkness, or smoke.

Communications At the start of World War II, the usual practice was to equip only the company commander's tank with a radio. All communications between tanks were by hand signals and flags. Today's tanks carry powerful radios with sufficient frequencies available for platoon, company, and battalion communication networks. Unit commander's tanks are also likely to be equipped with telefax machines, satellite links to rear areas for navigation and communication, and laser communication devices.

German armor, equipment, and the *blitzkrieg* style of battle. By the end of the Spanish Civil War in 1939 the German Army had not only built or planned a wide range of tank designs but had taken Fulton's tactics, which de Gaulle and Liddell Hart had expanded on, and made them work on a divisional scale.

If any one person can be singled out as the inventor of modern tank warfare, it is probably General Heinz Guderian. He not only understood how to use the tank but could communicate that understanding to his peers and superiors. Guderian maintained that tanks in massed formations should be thrown against weak points in the enemy line. Once the breakthrough occurred, it must be followed up immediately by mobile infantry to hold the ground the tanks had taken. His vision was realized for the first time on the plains of Poland in September 1939.

The United States After World War I, the United States had wrapped itself in a mantle of isolationism and virtually ignored its armed forces. Little money was available for the development of tanks, particularly since the United States limited its military efforts to police actions in its own hemisphere and the defense of its Pacific possessions. The United States had effectively forsworn the possibility of ever going to war overseas again—except against Japan. And until the mid-1930s, it was thought that a war against Japan would be strictly a naval war.

The Tanks Corps was disbanded in 1920 and its few tanks reassigned to the infantry. During the next 15 years, only 20 tanks were built in the United States, and they were essentially copies of the French Renault FT-17. American tank tactics followed the British pattern. Some cavalry regiments turned in their horses and were mechanized, but the tactics remained largely unchanged.

New Developments Developments were underway that would make the tank of World War II the most important asset of any land force. The first development was a new tank design by Vickers-Armstrong. They developed the Six Ton Tank, which carried a 47mm gun, a machine gun, and armor between 0.4 and 0.5 inch thick. The tank was fast, light, agile, and heavily gunned for its time. The British Army turned it down, but a few were sold to Russia, where it was slightly redesigned and manufactured as the T-26. Poland bought it as 7-TP, and it inspired the Czech LT-35 and LTH tanks and the Swedish Stridsvagn Model 1931.

The second significant development came from J. W. Christie's work with amphibious vehicles. He developed a simplified suspension system that could use either wheels or caterpillar tracks. A prototype tracked tank achieved 42 miles per hour, making it faster than the Vickers-Armstrong design. The United States Army experimented with the design in the T-3 and T-4 prototype tanks, then dropped them. The Soviets bought two Christie T-3s and from

this came their famous BT series. The BT-5, built in 1933, carried a high-velocity 45mm gun.

This light/medium-tank class was considered ideal in the mid-1930s because it could both support infantry and operate in the cavalry role. But the Spanish Civil War proved the light/medium tanks inadequate. When operating in support of infantry and moving at infantry pace, they were too lightly armored to withstand enemy antitank gunnery.

German designers responded with the Panzerkampfwagen (Pz.Kpfw) III and IV models, which were the mainstays of German armored forces until 1942. The Pz.Kpfw III, a light/medium tank, was given a 37mm gun (it was later up-gunned to 50mm). The Pz.Kpfw IV medium tank was given a 75mm gun, making it the most powerful tank in its class in the opening stages of World War II. The Pz.Kpfw IV operated primarily in support of the Pz.Kpfw III.

Disregarding the mobility of the light/medium tank, designers in France and Britain concluded that, to be effective, the infantry tank should carry heavier armor. The armor on France's new Renault R-35 was increased to 1.5 inches. The British added up to 2.3 inches on their new British Infantry Tank Mark I. The Mark I, or "Matilda" as it was nicknamed, was intended as a close infantry support tank and thus was armed with a .303 machine gun. It could travel at a maximum speed of 8.8 miles per hour. (This Mark I should not be confused with the Mark I of World War I; they were completely different tanks.)

A new cruiser tank—the British designation for tanks designed to exploit the breakthrough achieved by the infantry/infantry tank combination—was also being designed in the early 1930s. The cruiser tank variations culminated in the Mark III, which was based partly on the Soviet BT design with its Christie suspension and which carried a 40mm gun. But combat in the Spanish Civil War showed that such light/medium tanks needed the support of heavier and more heavily gunned and armored tanks.

The French Army issued a specification for a medium tank in the early 1930s. The tank, designed and built by SOUMA, was originally called the AMC SOUMA-3 but was renamed the Char SOUMA S-35 Medium Tank when it entered service. The S-35 was capable of 23 miles per hour and carried up to 2.2 inches of armor as well as a 47mm high-velocity gun. Some 500 had been built by the beginning of 1940.

While the Germans were considering up-gunning the light/medium Pz.Kpfw III in the late 1930s, the Soviets were at work on the new T-34 tank, which was to be equipped with a 76.2mm gun. The T-34 design can be traced back through the BT series to the Vickers-Armstrong Six Ton Tank, but it carried considerably

Right: The Vickers-Armstrong Six Ton Tank, shown here in interwar years camouflage, was ignored by the British Army. **Top left:** The Swedish Landsverk 30 of 1933 used treads for cross-country and wheels for operating on roads, a technique designed to prolong tread life. **Top right:** The British Cruiser Mark I had a top speed of 25 mph, a range of 150 miles, and was armed with a two-pounder gun and three machine guns. It served in France in 1940 and in Egypt through 1941.

heavier armor (1.75 inches). The T-34 was one of the first tanks to make use of sloped and rounded surfaces to increase armor protection yet keep the weight within reasonable bounds.

Heavy tanks were not neglected during this prewar period. The Soviet KV heavy-tank series carried nearly 3 inches of armor and a 76.2mm gun, but it was slow. The British had started designing the Infantry Tank Mark II, or the Matilda II, in 1937. It was given slightly thicker armor than the Mark I but, like cruisers, carried only a 40mm gun.

Italy and the United States were not even in the armor race in the mid-1930s. Italy had only 70 Model 11 tanks with 37mm guns. The rest of its 1,500 armored vehicles were L/3 Tankettes, little better than armored cars. The United States in 1940 had a few experimental tanks equipped with 37mm guns, but active service tanks were equipped with machine guns.

In the mid-1930s Japan had developed the Type 95 KE-GO Light Tank (more commonly known by its manufacturer's designation, HA-GO; KE-GO is the military designation), which was widely used in China, but only a few were armed with 37mm guns. Based on combat experience in China, the Japanese General Staff saw the need for a heavier tank with a more powerful gun. The result, after a runoff competition in the late 1930s, was the Mitsubishi Type 97 CHI-HA Medium Tank armed with a 57mm gun. The Type 97 and subsequent tanks were, and remained, inferior to anything the United States produced.

How World War II Was Won

The differences in tactical uses of the tank that soon appeared on the Polish, French, and Russian plains derived not so much from thickness of armor, caliber of gun, or speed, as from the way tanks were collectively used. As noted earlier, General Guderian had persuaded the German High Command to employ tanks in massed formation, closely followed by truck-borne infantry to hold the ground the tanks passed over. The concept differed little in theory from that held by the British. It was in practice that they were worlds apart.

In one sense, the German *blitzkrieg* ("lightning war") was a hoax. The tanks Germany used to sweep across Poland in three weeks during September 1939 were Pz.Kpfw Is and IIs because not enough Pz.Kpfw IIIs and IVs had yet been manufactured. The tanks often got so far ahead of their supporting infantry that there was no one for defeated soldiers to surrender to for hours or even days. The Pz.Kpfw I was armed only with machine guns, the Pz.Kpfw II with a 20mm cannon. But against Poland's few tanks, horse cavalry, and unmechanized infantry, they proved more than sufficient.

During the invasion of France nine months later, Guderian's armored forces consisted primarily of the Pz.Kpfw II with a sprinkling of Pz.Kpfw IIIs and IVs in support. Yet they outmaneuvered and destroyed the heavily armored British Matilda IIs and the more heavily armed French R-35s and S-35s. The entire German tank force during the 1940 invasion of France consisted of ten divisions containing 2,574 tanks. The French alone had a total of 3,800 tanks, most equal to or better than Germany's. But superior German tactics proved decisive.

Again, the following year massed tanks smashed Yugoslavia and Greece in six weeks and then turned and poured across European Russia, reaching the gates of Moscow before being turned back by winter, not the Red Army.

By 1943 German tanks were truly superior to Allied tanks and remained so to the end of the war. The Germans had learned quickly in the tank battles of 1942 that the Pz.Kpfw IV's 24 caliber 75mm gun was no match for the long-barrel 76.2mm guns mounted on the T-34 and KV-1. A long-barrel 75mm gun of 48 calibers (exactly double in length) was fitted to the new Pz.Kpfw IVF model and retrofitted to existing Pz.Kpfw IVs. The new, higher velocity gun gave the Pz.Kpfw IV the needed margin of superiority over the T-34. Similarly, armor was increased on succeeding models and retrofitted whenever possible.

In 1943 Germany introduced the Panther Pz.Kpfw V, a new medium tank designed to achieve definite superiority over Soviet tanks. The Panther incorporated the best elements of the T-34 design, including sloped armor of 4.72 inches, as well as a newly designed suspension system. Most important, however, was the new 70 caliber 75mm gun that fired an armor-piercing shell at a velocity of 3,070 feet per second—enough to penetrate 4.72 inches of sloped armor plate at 1,094 yards.

The Panther was rushed into production before design and testing were complete because Hitler wanted it to participate in the pivotal Battle of Kursk, which began on July 5, 1943. Kursk was perhaps the most important land battle in World War II; at its height, 3,000 German and Russian tanks occupied a narrow strip of territory just 15 miles wide. Its battle lines marked the high tide of German land conquest. Its finish nearly four weeks later saw the beginning of a long German retreat that ended at Berlin less than two years later.

The Battle of Kursk also marked a major tactical change in armored warfare. At Kursk, the Soviets constructed antitank defenses reaching back nearly 100 miles from the front lines. Enemy tanks were channeled into specific lanes on which artillery fire had been preregistered, mines laid, and antitank weaponry sited. And waiting for the survivors was Soviet armor.

Right: The Soviet heavy tanks at the beginning of WW II were the KV-1 and KV-1A, the latter mounting a 76.2mm gun. The heavily armored Soviet tanks first saw action in the Winter War against Finland in 1939–40. **Far right:** The Soviet KV-1 was nearly invulnerable to antitank fire in the early days of the invasion of Russia. A favorite German tactic was for several Pz.Kpfw IIIs or IVs to isolate a KV-1 and shell it repeatedly until the crew was killed or a shell found a soft spot.

The new Panthers were shipped directly from their factories to assembly points in Russia. Not all the bugs had been worked out, and along the way many Panthers had their engines and transmissions cannibalized, as well as machine guns, gun sights, and even tracks removed by armored units in the rear. Also, crews were given little time to familiarize themselves with the new tank.

The new Panther was thus at a terrible disadvantage, and most were destroyed in the first day's fighting. But later, when all the bugs were worked out, the Panther became the finest tank in the German Army. The American rule of thumb was that it took five Shermans to knock out one Panther.

The heavy tank's task changed as the war progressed. The Germans, convinced by their experiences in Spain, quickly made the necessary changes, while the British ignored them and the United States and the Soviet Union delayed introducing their own heavy tanks. By 1943 the heavy tank was supporting medium tanks in attack. It stood beyond the enemy's range and knocked out tanks with a long-range gun. The medium tanks then engaged the remainder and broke through the enemy defensive lines.

The Pz.Kpfw VI Tiger was the main German heavy tank. It weighed 56 tons and was armed with a powerful 88mm gun adopted from an 88mm antiaircraft gun. The original Tiger was replaced in 1944 with the Tiger II, or Royal Tiger, an even heavier (76.5 tons) and better armed and armored version of the Pz.Kpfw VI.

The Tiger II was not indestructible: Although virtually invulnerable to frontal attack by anything in the Allied inventory, it lacked agility and its road and cross-country speeds were low. But again, superior tactics made the difference. Tigers operated in units of four or five and worked best when lying in wait for an enemy tank column. Unless an enemy could get behind it and nail it through the thinner rear armor, the Tiger could rarely be knocked out. One Tiger I was said to have destroyed 24 American tanks before it was finally killed from behind.

The appearance of the Tiger finally galvanized the Soviets. They developed their prewar-designed KV series into the Joseph Stalin (JS or IS) tank. The first JS tanks carried an 85mm gun, but this was soon changed to the 122mm M1943, or D-25, main gun. At 50 tons, somewhat lighter than a Tiger, it was a bit more agile, and its powerful gun was a near match for the Tiger II's armor.

The Soviets, under stress, learned fast. The Soviet T-34 tank, after tantalizing appearances in the fall, burst onto the scene in the winter of 1942 in the battles that raged on the southern front. It was first gunned with a short-barrel 76.2mm weapon that was adequate against the more lightly armed Pz.Kpfw IIs, IIIs, and IVs. But the appearance of the Panther required up-gunning to a long-barrel 76.2mm gun and eventually to the 85mm M39 gun. Armor thickness grew as well, and while the T-34 could never slug it out gun-to-gun with the Panther, it remained a match for the German tank by superior agility, mobility, and just plain numbers.

Despite evidence of their ineffectiveness, the cruiser and infantry categories of specialized tanks were maintained by the British to the end of the war. As a result, British tanks lagged behind in armament for most of the war. When the Crusader III, a cruiser tank developed in the late 1930s and armed with a two-pounder gun, was reequipped with a 57mm gun in 1943, the Pz.Kpfw IV was already carrying a long-barrel 75mm gun. When the Churchill Infantry Tank, first deployed in 1941 and a replacement for the Matilda II, was armed with a 57mm gun, it was sent to face Tigers in North Africa equipped with 88mm guns. By the time 76mm guns were mounted in all British categories, they were still outgunned by Panthers and Tigers carrying 88mm guns.

American Efforts: From A Standing Start The United States started tank development almost from scratch. In 1931, Chief of Staff Douglas MacArthur canceled plans for a specialized armored corps and ordered the army to be mechanized. The cavalry was to take charge of all light tanks and use them in a reconnaissance role. In fact, to get around a congressional order that only infantry could use tanks, the cavalry's light tanks were called combat cars.

Although the United States had neither the money nor determination to maintain their armed forces nor a balanced understanding of world events, it had officers of vision like Colonels Adna R. Chaffee and George S. Patton, who understood the use of mechanized forces and were willing to learn new tactics. Chaffee and Patton formed the 7th Cavalry Brigade (mechanized) with 112 light tanks (combat cars). Combined exercises held in 1940 were covered so extensively by the media—especially *Life* magazine—that, combined with German successes in Poland and France, Congress was finally pressed into funding an armored force.

Almost too late, development and production of the M-2A2 tank (all of them equipped with machine guns except 18 that mounted a 37mm gun) was expanded. After May 1940 a 75mm gun was the standard tank gun, and the M-2 was redesigned to carry it. The result was the M-3 Medium Tank.

Work went quickly. In 1940 there were only 464 tanks in the entire army, but during that year 330 new tanks were built. The following year, 4,052 were built. In 1942, 24,977: more than Germany

Bottom: The Joseph Stalin heavy tank replaced the increasingly vulnerable KV-1A heavy tank. It first saw action in the spring of 1944. **Top, left to right:** The Crusader Mark VI (first two photos) was the main British tank in 1941–42. The Crusader arrived in North Africa in 1941 and participated in every major engagement until the Afrika Korps surrendered. The Churchill (second two photos) was the last of an illustrious line of infantry tanks built by the British between 1916 and 1945.

23

built during the entire war. In fact, by 1944 Germany had produced some 24,370 tanks. By contrast, the British, Americans, and Soviets had built a total of 170,790 tanks.

Lend Lease and America Enters the War In 1940 President Franklin Roosevelt, embroiled in a reelection battle and increasingly at odds with an isolationist Congress, knew he had to find a way to supply more military equipment and weapons to the British. Britain had been paying cash for whatever they got from the United States, but their gold reserves were nearly exhausted. The plan the President and his advisers hit upon was to lend 50 overage destroyers to Great Britain in exchange for American leases to British naval installations in the Western Hemisphere.

Once approved by Congress, Roosevelt interpreted the law in the most liberal manner possible. The destroyers went immediately into the North Atlantic on convoy and antisubmarine patrol. Hundreds of aircraft, thousands of tanks, and millions of tons of other military equipment soon followed.

The burst of industrial productivity triggered by the Lend Lease program pulled America out of the Great Depression and allowed it to tool up production capacity for the war against the three Axis Powers—Germany, Italy, and Japan—that President Roosevelt knew was inevitable. It also provided the United States with valuable tank construction experience.

M-3 and M-5 Stuart Light Tanks and M-3 Medium Tanks were supplied to Great Britain, the Soviet Union, and China in great quantities. The British in particular made excellent use of the M-3 Light Tank with its long-barrel 37mm gun, which they designated the Stuart but nicknamed "Honey" because of its handling characteristics and reliability. Honeys were too lightly armored to withstand antitank defenses, but their speed and maneuverability made them a good match against Rommel's early model Pz.Kpfw IIIs and IVs in North Africa.

When the United States entered the war in December 1941, the M-3 light and medium series were the only modern tanks in the Army's inventory, although not in appreciable quantities. An understanding of how they should be used came courtesy of British and Soviet tankers. During the opening stages of the American phase of the war, the independent armored divisions acted alone in massed formations and were shellacked by the experienced Germans. In 1943 a reorganization that combined aspects of the German, British, and Russian experiences began. United States armored divisions were reduced in tank numbers, and mechanized infantry and artillery support units were added. There were 52 armored divisions when the reorganization was completed in 1944. Generally, each division consisted of three tank battalions, with 219 tanks per division. Stronger and working

from a better tactical book, they roared out of the Normandy beachhead to meet and beat the German professionals at their own game.

The earlier M-2A4, which had been in production since 1939, was armed with a 37mm gun. It was used primarily in a training role, although a few found their way to Guadalcanal with the Marines.

The M-3 series of medium tanks was quickly supplemented by the M-4 Medium Tank, designated the Sherman. It was designed at Rock Island Arsenal, Illinois, and mounted the new M3 75mm gun. It first came off the production line in February 1942 and before production ended was being built in nine different plants in the United States. The nominal engine was a Wright R-975 aircraft engine, but a variety of engines, including two types of diesels, were used to maintain production rates.

When introduced, the M-4 could meet on equal terms any tank the Axis powers could field. M-4s were supplied to British forces in North Africa, and 270 were used at El Alamein. In fact, the M-4 Sherman became the standard British medium tank. Some 1,900 saw service from Normandy to the Elbe in British hands. And 4,000 were shipped to the Soviet Union. Later, new German tanks were introduced and older models up-gunned. New tactics were developed so Shermans could handle Panthers and Tigers until the arrival in mid-1944 of the more powerful M-4A3E8 with its 76mm gun. Still, at the beginning of 1945, it was estimated that three American tanks were being lost for every German tank.

The M-4 Sherman was quickly reworked with a new gun, appliqué armor (see sidebar "Tank Armament and Armor"), and other features to bring it up to M-4A3E8 standards. Another variation included the King Cobra (or Jumbo) model, a special assault tank designed for use during the breakout from the Normandy beachhead. It took its name from the breakout codeword, Operation Cobra. A total of 45,032 M-4s of all types were manufactured before the war ended.

The M-24 Light Tank, dubbed the Chaffee by the British, replaced the M-3/M-5 Light Tank series in 1943. Some 4,070 were built before the war ended. The 40 miles per hour Chaffee was a cavalry reconnaissance tank, although its long-barrel 37mm gun could inflict severe damage on medium tanks. Like the M-4, the M-24 served as the basic model for a range of specialized vehicles, including the M-18 Hellcat with a long-barrel 76mm gun. Its chassis was also used for the M-41 Howitzer Motor Carriage, which carried a 105mm howitzer.

The M-26 Pershing was the only true American heavy tank of World War II. It mounted a 53 caliber 90mm gun, had a road speed of 20 miles per hour, weighed 41 tons, and carried up to 4

Right: The M-18 Hellcat, which carried the 76mm M1A1 or M1A2 gun, is properly classified as a tank destroyer. The M-18 saw service in Europe in 1944–45 and later in Korea. It had thin armor and relied on its speed to stay out of trouble. **Top, left and right:** The M-2 Medium Tank was the first modern tank to enter production in the United States. More than 800 M-2 tanks of various configurations were built between 1938 and 1940. They were used for training and never saw combat.

inches in armor. A heavy-tank development program was in limbo when the United States Army came face to face with German Panthers and Tigers. Suddenly, a heavy tank was needed, pronto. Twenty M-26s arrived in Europe in January 1945, and they outmatched the Tiger II in every respect. By the end of the European phase of the war in May, some 200 were in service.

Japanese Armor   The Japanese tended to follow the British and American pattern of maintaining two classes of tanks, one to exploit breakthroughs and the other to accompany infantry. But overall, armor played a relatively minor role in Japanese tactical thinking except in China and, to some extent, in Burma and Malaya.

In the early 1930s the Japanese Army bought several British Vickers Six Ton Tanks and French Renault FTs for study. The first Japanese tank designed and built indigenously was the Number 1. In the Japanese year 2589 (1929) Japan built its first Type 89 medium tank. Starting in 1932, the 12.8 ton Type 89s were used in great numbers in China to support infantry operations. They were equipped with a 57mm gun and two 6.5mm machine guns.

To provide support and communications for the widely scattered garrisons in north China and Manchuria, the Type 94 Tankette, based on the British Carden-Loyd design, was developed. More an armored car than a tank, it was equipped with one 6.5mm machine gun and had .25 inch of armor that was protection against small arms fire only.

Manchuria is primarily dry uplands with few natural resources. Therefore, water for cooling engines as well as the economics of producing gasoline were always a consideration. Since more diesel fuel than gasoline could be produced from the same amount of crude oil, an air-cooled diesel engine was designed. From 1937 to the end of the war, this engine was used in all Japanese tanks. The Type 95 light tank, weighing 7.5 tons, was the first to be equipped with the new diesel engine. Designated the KE-GO in 1937, it saw action on every front. The KE-GO supported Japanese troops at the start of the main offensive into China in 1937; it was used against the Soviets at Khalkin-Gol during the Japanese–Soviet conflict in 1939; and it pushed the tide of Japanese conquests down the Malay Peninsula to Singapore in 1942. KE-GOs were encountered by American Marines and Army troops during every central Pacific and south Pacific island campaign.

The Type 97 SHINHOTO CHI-HA medium tank was well built and heavily armored for its time, but, as experience in the 1939 Japanese–Soviet conflict showed, it was lightly armed with a long-barrel 47mm gun. The tank was up-armed with a new 48mm gun in 1942. The Type 97 was distributed among armored regiments.

Each regiment contained three to four tank companies; each company comprised three platoons of three tanks each. Tanks were attached to a regimental headquarters as well. Depending on the theater and the local commander, Japanese tank regiments were used either very well, as at Jitra and the Slim River in Malaya, or very poorly, as in the Pacific Islands in 1943 and 1944 and the Philippines in 1945, where they were wasted in static defensive positions.

Japan built 6,400 tanks, 4,424 of them between 1941 and 1945. As a general rule, they were no match for American or Soviet armor. The problem was production and transportation rather than design, especially after 1944, when American submarines and bombers disrupted Japanese shipping and production. As a consequence, when Japanese armor was put to the test during the August 1945 Lightning War in Manchuria, the Type 95s and Type 97s were literally blown away by the Soviet T-34s armed with new 85mm guns. Using massed armor formations backed by mechanized infantry, the Soviets swept the Japanese out of Manchuria in less than six weeks.

The Postwar World and the Cold War

By 1945, Britain had rejected the concept of the infantry tank and was beginning to accept the idea that tanks had to be armed and armored to fight other tanks. Even so, British—and American—tanks were still being divided between armored and infantry units.

The Cold War in Europe, which began with the Berlin Blockade in 1948, and the invasion of South Korea by North Korea on June 25, 1950, galvanized tank development—both equipment and tactics—once again. The development of tactical nuclear weapons provided an additional impetus, since armored vehicles allowed troops to operate with a greater degree of safety on the nuclear battlefield.

Korea   If the lesson had not been learned during World War II, it was repeated again in Korea: The only truly effective counter to a heavily gunned and armored tank was another heavily gunned and armored tank. The North Koreans possessed an effective force of 85mm gunned T-34s, which they used with some skill. By coordinating the T-34s with mechanized infantry and close air support, North Korea destroyed half the South Korean Army in the first few days of fighting and drove United Nations forces to the southeast corner of the peninsula.

The United States was not ready to fight a major land war in Asia, and President Harry S Truman avoided that possibility by limiting American military objectives and convincing the United Nations to do the same. The principal American tank used in Korea

Clockwise from top left: The Japanese Type 94 Tankette was based on the British Carden-Loyd design; the Japanese Type 95 Light Tank was designed to accompany mechanized infantry; the Type 97 SHINHOTO CHI-HA was Japan's workhorse medium tank, first used against Soviet forces in Manchuria in 1939; the United States adopted the heavy tank late in WW II with M-26 Pershings arriving on Okinawa in 1945; the Type 89 Medium Tank was Japan's most ubiquitous tank used during WW II.

was the M-4A3E8 Sherman with a 76mm gun. It was equal to the 85mm gunned T-34, but again, as in World War II, superior numbers made the difference. The Chinese entered the war in 1951, when United Nations troops approached the Yalu River. The Chinese were essentially a guerrilla force equipped with a hodgepodge of American, Soviet, Japanese, and Chinese weapons, and few tanks.

Tank battles fought in Korea (and later in the Sinai between Egypt and Israel (1956, 1967, and 1973) and in Kashmir between India and Pakistan (1965 and 1971)) reinforced the lesson that once enemy tanks were defeated, friendly tanks could break through enemy defenses. Mechanized infantry could then take and hold ground. For the infantry to keep up with the tanks, the armored personnel carrier (APC), which had first made its appearance in the latter stages of World War II, grew into a class of armor all its own.

Vietnam   The tank did not play a major role in the Vietnam conflict. The terrain, dense vegetation, weather, and lack of enemy armor until after the United States had pulled its fighting forces from the country limited the tank's usefulness. The principal American tank in Vietnam was the M-48A3 Patton. It was equipped with a 90mm gun and weighed 47 tons. The M-551 Sheridan, equipped with a 152mm gun that could fire shells or missiles, was also used but much less successfully. The Sheridan was too light to power through mud and dense vegetation and too lightly armored to withstand North Vietnam Army (NVA) and Vietcong antitank missiles. Army of the Republic of Vietnam (ARVN) troops were equipped with the M-41A3 Walker Bulldog, a light tank originally designed for scouting in World War II.

ARVN Walker Bulldog tanks, accompanying armored personnel carriers, participated in the 1970 invasion of Laos. In 1971 the Walker Bulldog was also involved in Operation Lam Son 719, in which North Vietnamese tanks met ARVN armor. Slowed by mud, bomb craters, destroyed roads, and ARVN command indecision, the attack was a failure. Lam Son 719 marked the beginning of North Vietnam's shift to conventional war tactics. The NVA increased their use of long-range artillery to soften targets and then sent in tanks to overrun them, followed by regimental and larger size infantry attacks to take and hold ground.

Armament and Armor   Perhaps the two outstanding characteristics of tank development in the postwar world have been armament and armor. The "standard" armament found on a medium tank in 1945 was a 75mm gun of varying caliber capable of throwing an armor-piercing shot at a velocity of about 3,000 feet per second. After ignoring armament for so long, Britain led the way in up-gunning when it introduced the Centurion Mark 3 in 1948. The Centurion 3 carried an 83.4mm gun capable of firing

an armor-piercing, discarding sabot (APDS) shot at 4,800 feet per second that could punch through any armor then carried by any nation's tanks. In 1959, the Centurion was up-gunned with the 105mm gun.

At the same time, the British Army, adopting the German and Soviet approach of mixing heavy and medium tanks, began work on its new Conqueror, a 65-ton behemoth equipped with a 120mm gun. For every 42 Centurions per regiment, there were six Conquerors. The heavy tank provided long-range protection against enemy heavy tanks, much as the Tiger I and II had done for the Panthers. But, like the Tigers, their weight limited their mobility. By 1961 the Conqueror had been withdrawn from British service.

For the same reason, the Soviets also began to withdraw their heavy tanks, the JS-3 and the T-10 (a JS-3 with a 122mm gun). Instead, they concentrated on developing the "medium" tank. By the end of World War II, the T-34 had been improved with a heavier 85mm gun. An even more improved version, the T-44, had been designed and built, but not in quantity. The Soviets wanted a more powerful gun, and for that they needed a better-designed chassis and turret. The result was the T-54, built on the T-44 chassis but with an all-new turret that mounted a 100mm gun. The T-54 weighed only 36 tons and retained the mobility that was the hallmark of the T-34.

Birth of the Main Battle Tank

By 1963 Soviet military planners decided that a better armored, faster tank that could also carry a heavier gun was needed. The T-62 was introduced even while the T-54 was still being furnished to Soviet client states and customers around the world. The T-62 marks a watershed in armored history. For the first time, a tank was available that carried a sufficiently powerful gun (115mm) to knock out enemy tanks at heavy-tank range, yet was still agile enough at 42 tons to maneuver with medium tanks. The T-62 was the first of what came to be called the Main Battle Tank (MBT). It should be noted that communist nations are not forthcoming with technical information concerning their armor. In some instances, the best inferences of the Western military intelligence community must be relied upon.

In the immediate postwar years, the United States continued to build both heavy and medium tanks. The M-103 Heavy Tank, armed with a 120mm gun, was a follow-up to the M-26 Pershing. The M-46 Medium Tank was adopted in 1948. It was also based on the M-26 but was given a new engine and transmission. After the outbreak of the Korean War, when a heavier gun was required to deal with the 85mm gunned T-34, the M-103's turret was mounted on the M-46 to produce the M-47 Medium Tank.

Top left: The Conqueror was the last British heavy tank. **Top right:** The M-46 was the predecessor to the famous M-48 Patton. **Bottom left:** The M-551 Sheridan was designed and built as an Armored Reconnaissance/Airborne Assault Vehicle. **Bottom center:** The view from the commander's position in the turret shows that the interior of the M-551 Sheridan was even more cramped than that of most tanks. **Bottom right:** Toward the end of WW II, the Soviets produced a new medium tank, the T-44.

But the chassis of the M-47 was not sturdy enough. A whole new series of tanks was designed, the M-48 Patton. The M-48 was the first American MBT and eliminated any further need for a heavy-tank class. The M-48 has been widely distributed around the world and has been upgraded, up-gunned, and up-engined, especially in the hands of the Israelis. At least 12 official U.S. variations have been built and adopted, as well as countless foreign models. Total production equaled 11,703 units.

The M-48 and variations of the M-48A3 were built with a 90mm gun. The M-48A5 carried a 105mm gun. Weight grew from 48.7 tons to 54 tons. But for this weight penalty, the United States Army wanted more firepower, armor, speed, range, and better serviceability. The result was the M-60. A new turret, carrying the British-designed 105mm gun, was matched to an M-48 body, and diesel engines replaced the M-48's gasoline engines. Except in weight, the M-60 proved superior to the M-48. The M-60 entered service in 1960. In 1962, the M-60A1 version with a redesigned turret was standardized.

In 1972 the Soviets began production of a new MBT, which was designated the T-64 by NATO. The new tank was a "luxury" model MBT. It had full nuclear-biological-chemical protection for the crew, a new five-cylinder diesel engine, and a redesigned T-62 turret. It also carried a powerful new 125mm gun with an automatic loader. This latter feature allowed the Soviets to dispense with a human loader. Doing so not only eliminated one crewmember but also allowed a smaller, more compact tank, since the loader has to stand upright inside the tank to lift the heavy shells from their storage compartment into the breech. The T-64 was a new MBT design that confused Western intelligence, but it was not as successful as its Soviet designers had anticipated. Problems with the automatic loader, the engine, and fire control system led the Soviets to end T-64 production in 1981.

Production of the T-72, a vastly improved version of the T-64, began in the early 1970s. Like the T-64, the T-72 used an automatic loader to feed its 125mm main gun. Armor that is lighter than that carried by British or American tanks keeps its weight to 45.2 tons and gives it a road speed of 43 miles per hour.

In 1980 a variant of the T-72 was designated the T-80. The T-80 is considered an up-rated T-72. It was given a new turret that mounted a smoothbore 125mm gun. A gas turbine engine replaced the T-72's V-12 diesel. The tank is thought to have received a modernized fire control system. The T-64/T-72/T-80 fleet of MBTs compose the mainstay of the Soviet/East Bloc armored fleet but the T-62 and the T-55 and their variants remain in service.

The United States moved early to meet the challenge of the T-64/T-72/T-80 series of Soviet MBTs. As noted above, the M-60 was upgraded to the M-60A1, then to the M-60A3 with an improved fire control system that included a laser range finder, computers, and a thermal night sight.

In the late 1960s, the United States and West Germany agreed to jointly develop an MBT. It was christened the MBT 70. But a combination of different service requirements and national pride caused the program to be canceled. The West Germans proceeded with the program and produced the Leopard 2. The United States developed the M-1 Abrams series, which entered service at Fort Hood, Texas, in 1981.

The initial M-1 Abrams MBT was equipped with the same 105mm gun used for the M-60 series. But in 1985, the first M-1A1s were delivered with an improved fire control system and the West German 120mm smoothbore gun. Like the Soviet T-64/T-72/T-80 series, the M-1 Abrams series features full nuclear-biological-chemical protection for its crew.

The British were also busy during the 1960s and 1970s. The Arab–Israeli wars were fought in what has been referred to as ideal tank country—open desert or rolling hills. The four campaigns—1956, 1967, 1973, and the 1982 invasion of Lebanon—have been carefully studied by military analysts around the world. Those experiences have been incorporated into the Soviet and American MBT concept. The British, while accepting those lessons, have decided that the heavy tank, with its long-range firepower, still has an important role to play on the modern battlefield.

Accordingly, in 1970, the British began work on a new heavy tank to replace the Chieftain. The result was the Challenger MBT. Weighing 68 tons, it is one of the heaviest tanks ever built. The Challenger mounts the 120mm L11A5 main gun, and its diesel engines can maintain a road speed of 37 miles per hour, which is slower than the M-1A1 Abrams or the T-64/T-72/T-80 series.

Sweden decided in the mid-1950s to develop its own battle tank. It wanted a tank that could carry a large main gun yet be light enough to operate on the tundra that composes so much of Swedish territory. The result was the Stridsvagn 103B, or S tank, a relatively light 43-ton, turretless tank equipped with a 105mm gun and an automatic loader. In 1984 a modernization plan began that will be completed by 1990.

Today, the standard armored formation is a mechanized tactical unit comprising tanks, infantry in armored personnel carriers, and self-propelled guns and rocket launchers, all supported by air power. Tank battles fought in the Middle East since 1956 have served to confirm and refine the design of the Main Battle Tank through the 1990s. They have also set the stage for the next class of tanks that will enter service in the 21st century.

Right: The MBT 70 was a joint development program between West Germany and the United States to develop a common MBT. Different requirements and national desires caused the dissolution of the program in January 1970. However, from the prototype MBT 70, shown here, both the Leopard and the M-1 Abrams ultimately evolved.

Tank Armament and Armor

Armament When the concept of the tank was first realized in 1915, machine guns or a light cannon were thought sufficient armament for infantry support. It quickly became apparent that heavier guns were needed, both to clear the way through heavily defended enemy positions and to engage enemy tanks.

At the beginning of World War II, guns of 37 millimeter to 57mm were considered adequate, particularly since large tank-to-tank battles were not envisioned and armor was relatively thin. But as heavier tanks with greater armor protection appeared, tank guns gained in power.

Tank gun efficiency depends on two factors: the diameter of the round and the round's velocity. The heavier and faster a round is, the more powerful it is. Tank gun size is expressed in diameter and caliber. For example, a 57mm gun of 45 calibers is more powerful than a 57mm gun of 21 calibers. Caliber is determined by dividing the length of gun by the bore diameter. Thus a 57mm gun with a 3.92-foot-long barrel has a caliber of 21, while a 57mm gun with an 8.4-foot-long barrel has a caliber of 45. Longer gun barrels provide increased velocity because more propellant can be burned as the shell travels up the barrel, giving the projectile more acceleration.

As tank designers sought to improve survivability through thicker armor, armament designers developed increasingly powerful guns. Eventually, the tank became so large and heavy that it lacked the agility to maneuver on the battlefield. Other factors entered into the equation as well. The larger the gun, the larger the ammunition. The Tiger II, with its 88mm gun capable of firing a shell at a velocity of 3,340 feet per second, could carry 84 rounds, but the U.S. M-103 Tank Destroyer could hold only 34 rounds for its 120mm gun. Also, the M-103's ammunition was so long and heavy that projectile and powder charge had to be loaded separately, slowing the rate of fire.

The solution was to develop more effective munitions. At the start of World War II, all tank ammunition intended for tank-to-tank engagements used a solid projectile and was referred to as armor-piercing, or AP. The next step was to reduce the diameter of the solid projectile and surround it with a soft jacket. This increased kinetic energy on impact because the solid core drove through the soft jacket and concentrated its energy against a smaller area. This armor-piercing, composite, rigid ammunition (APCR) was first used in the German Pz.Kpfw III's 50mm gun in 1941.

In the United States, similar ammunition was called hyper-velocity, armor-piercing shot (HVAP) and, when fired from the British Sherman's VC Firefly 76mm gun, could achieve velocities of 4,100 feet per second in 1945. In 1944 the British developed a different round for the Churchill Infantry Tank's 57mm gun. It used soft metal jackets, called sabots, that fell away from the solid core after the round left the gun—armor-piercing, discarding sabot (APDS). The disadvantage for both types of ammunition was the drastic falloff in velocity as range increased.

Velocities increased dramatically when smoothbore, rather than rifled, guns were introduced in the 1950s. The smoothbore gun avoids the velocity lost due to friction created as the lands (raised, curving ridges that give the round its spin) of the barrel engrave the round. The smoothbore round fits snugly in the barrel to contain the propellant gases and uses pop-up fins after leaving the muzzle to stabilize itself in flight.

As velocity limits were reached in reasonably sized guns, attention turned to the round's effect. The high-explosive, antitank round (HEAT) does not depend on kinetic energy for effect. Rather it focuses the power of its explosive in a "shaped-charge." The HEAT round has a conical cavity lined with copper and backed with explosive that produces a jet of molten copper that can reach velocities of 27,000 feet per second or faster. The gas jet literally punches through armor. HEAT rounds are also very effective when used in such one- and two-crew portable antitank weapons as bazookas, recoilless rifle rounds, and antitank missiles.

Armor As the efficiency of tank guns—as well as antitank weaponry—increased, armor makers struggled to keep up. The British Mark I through VIII tanks of World War I carried .25-inch-thick boiler-plate had given way to cold-rolled steel. Designers also found that armor tilted at an angle to the incoming round was far more effective. The British Chieftain has 4.6 inches of armor sloped at 60° from the vertical. That 60° tilt makes 4.6 inches as effective as 9 inches of armor standing vertically.

Appliqué armor—additional plate bolted on to the tank—was introduced in 1943. A variation on this is spaced armor plate, which is appliqué armor with an air gap between it and the main armor. Spaced armor plate is effective against HEAT rounds because the main energy of the gas jet is dissipated by the appliqué armor and does not reach the main armor.

In the 1960s a new type of armor plate was developed in Chobham, England. Named after the area, Chobham armor is a mix of ceramic, plastic, and steel plates of varying hardness; the exact composition is a closely guarded secret. The American M-1 Abrams, the British Chieftain and Challenger, the West German Leopard 2, and the Soviet T-64/T-72/T-80 series all use Chobham-type armor.

The Israelis are credited with developing reactive armor, which is effective against shaped-charge warheads. Steel boxes are lined with explosives that detonate under impact and disrupt the shaped-charge's plasma jet. They also disrupt kinetic energy penetrator rods by deflection.

The newest development in armor is a combination of depleted (nonradioactive) uranium and steel. Depleted uranium is extremely dense and is considered very effective against both shaped-charges and penetrator rounds.

Tanks of the 21st Century

Ever since the invention of the first portable antitank rocket/missile, so-called experts have predicted the demise of the modern battle tank. In recently published writings, as well as those dating back to the end of World War I, tanks have been called everything from outdated leviathans to steel dinosaurs waiting to fall into the proverbial tar pits. Despite all the "expert" predictions, the modern battle tank has not fallen into extinction but actually is about to undergo a host of revolutionary changes that will keep it current and formidable on the battlefields of tomorrow.

"Tank 2000" will be a highly automated piece of machinery that will likely sport only a crew of two compared with the standard crew of three to five needed today. It will be lighter, faster, and lower. Unlike the Main Battle Tanks of today that can tip the scales at 70 tons or more, the future tank will have a maximum weight between 45 and 50 tons and have a top-end road speed of nearly 50 miles per hour and a "rough terrain" speed of up to 30 miles per hour. Today's tank can travel only 35 miles per hour on the open road and often not much more than 20 to 25 miles per hour in the dirt.

The new tank will hug the ground and stand little more than five feet tall compared with the eight foot tall tanks of today. Gone forever will be the familiar turret, the tank's hallmark since its introduction. To lower the tank's profile and decrease the chance of being hit, the turret will be replace by a swivel plate that nestles the gun in a low-slung cradle. The commander and the gunner will sit deep in the tank hull in a side-by-side configuration. Eliminating the turret also decreases the tank's weight by more than ten tons; this, along with smaller but much more powerful engine designs, adds measurably to increased fuel economy.

To look out and scan the battlefield of the future, a 30-foot mast rises up out of the tank. On the mast is a video camera that uses sophisticated imagery to cut through smoke, fog, snow, rain, and darkness to see what lies ahead, to either side, and behind. With infrared heat seekers, multiple magnification telescopes, and a warning system similar to that found on fighter planes, the tank crew will monitor what is occurring outside the metal/composite hull via a host of television screens located on the dashboard.

To see, steer, and navigate while buttoned up, the crew will be able to view the countryside in front of them through a real-life image projected on a screen. They'll also control a host of satellite or surrogate vehicles in addition to their own. These smaller robot tanks will be sent ahead of the mother tank and will be controlled electronically by the mother tank. The convoy of tiny tanks will carry everything from rockets to such small kinetic energy weapons as rail guns and will be the first line of defense against a

possible enemy attack or ambush. Thus the tank commander will be in charge of all navigation and weapons systems.

All tanks will use electromagnetic cannons that are state-of-the-art kinetic energy weapons (KEW). Instead of firing conventional tank rounds packed with high explosives, the KEW cannon, using a giant pulse of electromagnetic energy, fires a 25-pound lucite plastic or aluminum projectile. Conventional tanks fire rounds that travel at 3,000 feet per second, but the KEW projectile will race out at 10,000 to 15,000 feet per second and will effortlessly cut through targets up to three miles away. Long-range laser designators will not only spot the enemy tank but instantly calculate its exact range, speed, necessary lead for a shot, and other factors. Since no gunpowder or conventional explosives are used, the deadly round can be fired without the telltale signs of smoke or explosive boom. With electronic masking devices, it will be difficult for enemy tanks to determine exactly where the tank is located.

The designers of the futuristic tank will also borrow ideas from experts in submarine warfare and air combat. Today's modern submarine uses a host of sophisticated decoying techniques that give off submarinelike noises that draw away enemy torpedoes. Tank 2000 will use the same techniques and may even travel with an inexpensive decoy tank that uses older high-heat engines to defeat the enemy's sound, heat, and visual detectors and draw away enemy fire.

To further conceal itself from enemy attack, Tank 2000 will incorporate stealth technology similar to the coatings and materials used by the United States Air Force on the B-2 bomber. Special coatings on composite materials will reduce the tank's radar signature, while new cooling systems will chill the hot exhaust gases and then vent them downward and away from the tank. This will give heat-seeking missiles much more difficulty in locating their intended targets; many will simply burrow into the ground and explode harmlessly.

Ammunition will sport a computer bar code on each round, much like those a supermarket uses at the check-out counter to register item and price. This bar code will enable the tank to count its ammunition and automatically relay its supply status back to the supply depot or headquarters. Valuable wartime resources will not be wasted sending out an ammo carrier with 50 rounds to resupply a tank that needs only three, and the logistics of keeping a tank in a battle longer will be greatly simplified.

Tanks will make much greater use of electronics, computers, and artificial intelligence. While tanks won't be able to think at a level that would replace the crew, sensors will be able to interpret

Right: One of the major threats facing armored vehicles today or tomorrow centers on "pop-up" aircraft. Tanks of the future will use exotic weaponry, such as kinetic energy rail guns or laser beams, to defend themselves against this threat.

When it's time to service the tank, modular designs will enable near immediate replacement of all major components. Self-diagnostic troubleshooting systems will tell the maintenance specialists what needs to be repaired, fixed, or replaced. Fuel will be stored in spongelike containers outside the vehicle that can be dropped in case of a hit or when empty. With the modular fuel system, full tanks can be clipped on in a matter of seconds. In addition to allowing room for more ammunition and electronic gear, the danger of fire—the number one tank destroyer—will effectively have been eliminated and armor requirements greatly reduced.

Today, most tankers feel that the giant metal behemoths are anything but user friendly. In the most recent tests conducted by the United States Army, volunteers could tolerate no more than approximately 20 hours of confinement in the Abrams tank or Bradley fighting vehicle. Studies show that a crew may have to remain in their tank for several days on the battlefield of the future to avoid fallout or residue contamination from chemical or biological weapons. In Tank 2000, the crew of two will be able to stay buttoned up for nearly three times that long due to innovative designs that take human elements and factors into consideration.

Creature comforts, such as body-molded recliner seats with built in massagers, will become standard equipment. Elastic exercise cords hung from horizontal bars will allow the soldiers to exercise each of the major muscle groups while on picket duty or routine patrol. Relaxation tapes, including what the Army calls "sleep-inducing imagery," as well as music tailored to each crewmember's taste, will be available through helmet headphones. High-energy meals that are self-heating upon opening the package will provide the crew's main table fare.

Electronic sensors will provide security out to four miles while the crew rests or sleeps. If the sensors are triggered, an electronic voice identifies the threat and its direction and suggests possible escape/retaliatory action. Modeled after voice systems used in automobiles today, the system will also warn the crew of any mechanical shortcomings or problems. Early testing shows that most tankers like the general idea.

Tank 2000 will be as radically different from the modern M-1A1 Abrams MBT as the M-1A1 is from the British World War I tank, Big Willy. As the centerpiece on the battlefield since the end of the "war to end all wars," the tank has been the pivotal reason for either victory or defeat in countless battles over the past 70 years. Despite those who say the combat environment is no place for large pieces of armor, military experts and soldiers know that it will be several generations before anyone can say it's time to play taps for the battle tank.

video camera images the tank sees and connect them with a radar device that will look out for dangerous obstacles. Signals can then be sent to the tank's suspension to adjust the springs and tracks to take the strain or jolt of everything from a tank-trap ditch to climbing over a wall or concrete barrier.

Like the Top Gun pilots of the skies, who rely heavily on computers to lock on their weaponry, the crew of Tank 2000 will have computers on board that will aim the guns. The gunner will use thermal imaging equipment to pick up visual references or heat emissions from the enemy tanks around him, or he'll take enemy tank location readings from high-flying reconnaissance aircraft or secret spy satellites positioned overhead. Each time he locks onto a target, the gunner will press a button and the computer will remember the target's location, while the gun swings around to fire at it. If there are multiple targets, the computer will prioritize the threat and lock onto several enemy tanks simultaneously. In the automatic fire mode, the tank that poses the greatest threat will be taken out first, followed by the second, then the third, and so on. Loading of ammunition will be automatic, and the rate of fire will be as high as 80 rounds per minute for up to four minutes nonstop.

where a new radio was fitted, enabling all tanks in a unit to communicate with each other. A long M6 gun, first used in the M-3A1, was fitted. All these changes increased the M-5's weight by a little more than one ton, but the twin Cadillac engines gave it the same 36 miles per hour road speed as the M-3A1 series. British experience prompted the addition of sand shields and a new dual traverse system that allowed the gunner to fire the machine gun while he was traversing the turret—a feature especially helpful when dueling with antitank guns.

The M-5 was shipped to Great Britain in 1943 and 1944 and was used widely during and after the breakout from the Normandy beachhead. M-5s traveled with American and British troops into Germany. The tank also served as the basis for a range of special-purpose armored vehicles: the M-5 Command Tank; the M-5A1 Psychological Warfare vehicle, fitted with a loudspeaker system; the M-5A1 Cullin Hedgerow Cutter, used to scoop up beach obstacles and cut through the tough hedgerows in Normandy; three flamethrower variations; and a recon-

naissance vehicle. The most successful nontank variation was the M-8 Howitzer Motor Carriage, which mounted a 75mm Pack Howitzer for close infantry support.

The M-3/M-5 series proved adequate in service and was liked by the British but by mid-1943 the Stuart had shown that the day of the light tank had clearly passed. Stuarts were too lightly armored, and their 37mm M6 gun was not powerful enough to deal with the armor plate mounted on the German Pz.Kpfw III, Pz.Kpfw IV, and Pz.Kpfw V Panther.

M-3 Stuart (Honey) Light Tank	
Country:	United States of America
Type:	Light Tank
Dimensions	
Length:	4.53 m (14.8 ft)
Width:	2.23 m (7.3 ft)
Height:	2.51 m (8.2 ft)
Combat weight:	12,428 kg (13.7 tons)
Engine:	Continental W-670 250 hp gasoline
Armament:	One 37mm M5 or M6 main gun; up to four .30 caliber Browning machine guns
Crew:	4
Speed:	58 km/h (36 mph)
Range:	112 km (70 mi)
Obstacle/grade performance:	0.6 m (2 ft)
Date of service:	1941

M-5 Light Tank	
Country:	United States of America
Type:	Light Tank
Dimensions	
Length:	4.53 m (14.8 ft)
Width:	2.23 m (7.3 ft)
Height:	2.28 m (7.5 ft)
Combat weight:	15,290 kg (16.8 tons)
Engine:	Twin Cadillac V-8 220 hp gasoline
Armament:	One 37mm M6 main gun; two .30 caliber Browning machine guns; one .50 caliber Browning machine gun
Crew:	4
Speed:	58 km/h (36 mph)
Range:	160 km (99 mi)
Obstacle/grade performance:	0.45 (1.5 ft)
Date of service:	1942

Left: This M-3 Light Tank is equipped with extra fuel tanks, which greatly increases its range. **Right:** The M-3 Light Tank was "a honey of a tank" that first saw battle in North Africa in July 1941 with British forces.

M-3 Grant/Lee Medium Tank

Following the First World War, America, shocked by the slaughter of trench warfare and the vindictiveness with which the French and British persecuted the new moderate government in Germany, withdrew into a shell of isolationism that would endure until Japan attacked on December 7, 1941.

Few in Washington could foresee the possibility of the United States ever going to war again to protect European interests. The result of this thinking was the National Defense Act of 1920, which gutted the armed services. Only the Navy was seen to have a role in extraterritorial warfare, and that role was directed primarily at the Japanese. Even the Navy was dealt a near mortal blow by various acts of Congress that prevented or slowed the development of the aircraft carrier, the submarine, and the amphibious vehicle. The Washington Naval Treaty of 1923 even limited the number and size of large capital battleships that could be built.

The National Defense Act disbanded the armored corps and placed the tank with the infantry, thus relegating both light and medium tanks to the infantry support role. The heavy tank class was eliminated. Not until Hitler came to power in Germany and gobbled up Austria, the Sudetenland, and Czechoslovakia, did the United States begin to awake to the danger in Europe. Even then, isolationist sentiment remained so strong that President Franklin Roosevelt was forced to resort to various stratagems to rearm the country in the face of stiff congressional opposition.

Except for a few T-4s in 1935–36, no medium tank had been produced in the interwar period. In 1938 designers at Rock Island Arsenal, Illinois, the center for American tank design and, until 1940, tank production, developed the T-5, a radically new medium tank design. It used a radial engine developed by the Wright Continental Company for aircraft

use, a new type of suspension system in which three pairs of road wheels per side were mounted on bell cranks, and a front drive sprocket. It was equipped with a 37 millimeter main gun and two .30 caliber machine guns. Once adopted, it was designated the M-2 and underwent numerous upgrades. Rapid advances in tank design in Germany and Russia made the M-2 obsolete, and it was relegated to a training tank.

The invasion of Poland, the British experience in the desert, and the invasion of France all showed that a 37mm gun was not powerful enough to deal with enemy tanks. While German Pz.Kpfw IIIs and Pz.Kpfw IVs were still racing across the French countryside in early June 1940, demands were made on the U.S. Ordnance Department for a heavier tank gun. In August 1940 General Adna R. Chaffee, the commander of the new Armored Force, met with representatives from the Ordnance Department to final-

Left: The M-3 Medium Tank was armed with a 75mm main gun in a side sponson, a 37mm gun in the turret, and up to four 3.0 caliber Browning machine guns. **Right:** The M-3 Medium Tank carried a crew of six, five of whom are shown here adding Colt revolver and tommy gun power to the tank's formidable 75mm and 37mm guns. **Top right:** This M-3 Medium Tank undergoes testing in California's Mojave Desert in 1941.

ize plans to produce the M-2A1 Medium Tank. During the meeting, he demanded and received agreement to build a tank capable of carrying a 75mm gun.

The M-2 Medium Tank chassis and hull could not support a larger turret or absorb the recoil forces from a 75mm gun. To speed the new tank into production, a design compromise was reached. The new tank would mount a 75mm gun in a limited traversing sponson on the right side of a heavier chassis and hull from a previous experimental tank. Thus, even while the Detroit Arsenal—the factory intended to build the M-2 Medium Tank—was itself being built, the M-2 was canceled, and a new contract for the M-3—for which design work had not yet been completed—was issued.

The M-3 thus evolved from the M-2, but indirectly. Central to the M-3's production was a new tank factory—the Detroit Arsenal. In 1939, when it was clear that the United States would have to rearm, Ordnance sought to place contracts for tank production with existing heavy industrial companies. But William Knudson, president of General Motors Corporation and a member of the National Defense Advisory Commission (NDAC), pointed out that heavy industrial firms, such as the builders of railroad cars and generators, were inexperienced in mass production, particularly the overwhelming quantities that would soon be needed. His arguments persuaded the NDAC, and they in turn persuaded the Army. The Detroit Arsenal was commissioned specifically to build tanks. The facility was built in six months on 113 acres of land in Warren, Michigan. It was the largest manufacturing facility built to that time, and it was operated by Chrysler Motors.

In its most widely produced form, the M-3 used a cast-and-welded hull that was versatile enough that a diesel rather than an aircraft engine could be fitted when the latter was in short supply. One ver-

sion—the M-3A4—even had four Chrysler automobile engines combined in one power pack and was referred to as the "eggbeater." The M-3's armor plate of 1.45 inches maximum was considered adequate when the design was finalized in 1940. The M-3 was heavily armed: a .30 caliber Browning machine gun in a rotating cupola atop the turret, two more .30 caliber Browning machine guns mounted in the tank's bow, a 37mm auxiliary gun in the revolving turret plus a coaxial .30 caliber Browning machine gun, and a 75mm M2 or M3 main gun mounted in a sponson on the tank's right side. The main gun could fire either armor-piercing or high-explosive ammunition.

M-3 nomenclature is confusing. There is an M-3 Light Tank (the Stuart, a.k.a. Honey), and the M-3 Medium Tank is known as both the Grant and the Lee in British service. The first tanks purchased by the British Tank Commission were built by the Pullman and Pressed Steel Company, an American company, and carried a British-designed turret. These were known as the M-3 Grant I. All subsequent deliveries were made under the Lend Lease program. The M-3 standard with an American-designed turret was named the Lee I; the M-3A1 the Lee II, the M-3A3 the Lee III, the M-3A4 the Lee IV, and the M-3A3 with a diesel engine, the Lee V. The M-3A5 was called the Grant II.

The M-3 Grant I first saw action against the Germans at Gazala, North Africa, in May 1942. Initial problems with ammunition fuses kept the Grants from being quite as effective as the British wished, but it was clear that the 75mm gun certainly tended to even things up against the Pz.Kpfw IIIs and Pz.Kpfw IVs. In November of the same year, the M-3 weighed heavily in the scales against the Afrika Korps at El Alamein.

Although widely used in North Africa by British and Canadian forces and on the eastern front by the Soviets, the M-3 was

relatively short-lived. It was declared obsolete in March 1944, although it had been so considered from the introduction of the M-4 Sherman in April 1943. Nevertheless, the M-3, America's first medium tank to see combat, gave an excellent account of itself and enabled the British to push the German and Italian armies out of the Western Desert. This ended the threat to the Suez Canal, the possibility of a Nazi breakthrough into the Middle East, and an ultimate hookup with Japanese forces in southern Asia.

M-3 Grant/Lee Medium Tank

Country:	United States of America
Type:	Medium Tank
Dimensions	
Length:	5.64 m (18.5 ft)
Width:	2.72 m (8.9 ft)
Height:	3.12 m (10.2 ft)
Combat weight:	27,216 kg (30 tons)
Engine:	Wright Continental radial air-cooled 9 cylinder gasoline
Armament:	One 75mm M2 or M3 main gun; one 37mm M5 or M6 auxiliary; four .30 caliber Browning machine guns
Crew:	6
Speed:	42 km/h (26 mph)
Range:	193 km (120 mi)
Obstacle/grade performance:	0.6 m (2 ft)
Date of service:	1941

Right: These three American M-3 Medium Tanks are moving in "line astern," a descriptive phrase adopted from nautical terminology. **Top right:** An M-3 Medium Tank driver peers through the raised driver's hatch, which is in the hull just below, and to the left of, the 37mm turret gun.

The M-4 Sherman Medium To
mainstay of American armo
during World War II and the K
It saw service on every front: N
northern Europe, the eastern
the Pacific campaigns. Except
viet T-34, it probably had a gr
on the course of the war than
tank, light, medium, or heavy

One day after the M-3 Medi
always considered an interir
was ordered into productio
work started on a new mediu
overcome the deficiencies of th
main differences lay in increa

feet per second. Starting in August 1942, work on a new 76mm gun wavered until finally, in early 1943, the Armor Board approved its installation on new M-4s. In late 1942 tests were conducted on an M-4 armed with a 105mm howitzer. The tests proved so successful that more than 4,600 105mm armed M-4s were built.

The M-4's armor was the thickest that had ever been applied to an American tank until that time. It ranged from 3 inches on the turret front to a little less than 2 inches on the hull front to .25 inch on the top of

the hull. Armor was later supplemented by appliqué armor. Tank crews found dozens of ingenious ways to supplement the M-4's armor with chunks of timber, additional steel plates, and elaborate racks and fences holding sandbags.

As a result of relatively thin armor and the inferior design of ammunition storage, early M-4s tended to catch fire easily. To reduce the problem, ammunition storage racks were set lower in the hull and surrounded by jackets containing a water-glycerin mixture. The two-piece

howitzer ammunition was enclosed by armor plating.

The M-4 entered service in late 1942, and its 75mm gun, which could punch through 2.5 inches of sloped armor, was a match for anything that Germany and Japan could field. When the up-gunned M-4 with the 76mm gun appeared on the scene in 1944, it could penetrate a little more then 4 inches of armor sloped at 30° at a distance of 500 yards. The Pz.Kpfw V Panther carried 3.14 inches maximum of armor.

Left: This Sherman tank of the 10th Armored Division, 3rd Army, battles a Nazi strong point in Trier, Germany, in March 1945. **Right:** An M-4 Sherman in 1944 with rocket launchers.

U.S.ARMY 3058832

The M-4 probably went through more modification and experimentation than any other American tank until that time. Suffice it to say that the M-4 Sherman—named by the British—was the most widely produced tank of the war, including the Russian T-34. A total of 49,230 Shermans were built.

A wide variety of main armament was mounted on the M-4, including flamethrowers, rockets, 155mm guns, and 204mm howitzers. A variety of tank destroyers were also built and armed with 76mm and 90mm main guns and heavier armor. The M-4 was also used as a mine-clearance vehicle when equipped with flails and rollers. The most spectacular of these was the M-1 Aunt Jemima mine-clearance device that could be attached to the M-4. The Aunt Jemima was a mechanical roller consisting of ten ten-foot-diameter steel wheels divided into two pairs. They were chain driven by the M-4's front drive sprocket and rolled ahead of the tank. The unit was very effective for clearing mined roads, but it was so heavy a second M-4 often had to push the first.

The M-4 saw service with a variety of United Nations forces during the Korean War, where it met the T-34 for the first time in battle. The M-4 was used by both sides in the Indo–Pakistani War of 1965 and by Egyptian and Israeli forces in 1948, 1956, and 1967. The Israelis purchased many Shermans on the international arms market in the 1950s and received more from the United States in the form of military aid. Many were converted to Super Shermans and Ishermans with more powerful engines and heavier armor and main guns. Thousands of Shermans were distributed by the United States as military aid to friendly countries.

M-4 Sherman Medium Tank	
Country:	United States of America
Type:	Medium Tank
Dimensions	
Length:	6.27 m (20.6 ft)
Width:	2.67 m (8 ft)
Height:	3.37 m (11 ft)
Combat weight:	31,554 kg (34.7 tons)
Engine:	Ford GAA V-8 500 hp gasoline
Armament:	One 75mm M3 or 76mm M4 main gun; two .30 caliber Browning machine guns; one .50 caliber Browning machine gun
Crew:	5
Speed:	42 km/h (26 mph)
Range:	160 km (99 mi)
Obstacle/grade performance:	0.6 m (2 ft)
Date of service:	1942

Left: The M-4 Sherman was barely a match for the German Pz.Kpfw V Panther. Its 75mm gun could penetrate the Panther's side and rear armor only. Later versions of the Sherman carried a more powerful 76mm gun. **Right:** The M-4E4 flamethrower tank. The flamethrower was a field retrofit kit that replaced the hull machine gun.

 M-24 Chaffee Light Tank

The M-24 Chaffee Light Tank grew out of British experience in North Africa with the M-3 Stuart. The light tank's agility and speed was very desirable, but the M-3/M-5 series was too lightly gunned to be of much value after Germany introduced the Pz.Kpfw III, Pz.Kpfw IV, and Pz.Kpfw V Panther.

In April 1943 design studies began for a new light tank that would retain the best features of the M-3/M-5 but couple them to a heavier gun. The lightweight 75 millimeter M6 gun developed for the B-25 Mitchell attack bomber was selected. Its short recoil mechanism was ideally suited for the close confines of a tank's turret.

The Cadillac Division of General Motors, which had been so instrumental in the development of the M-5 Light Tank, was chosen as the major designer. They first tested the 75mm M6 gun on the M-8 Howitzer Motor Carriage—which used the M-5 hull and chassis. The concept worked, but the M-5's hull and chassis were not large enough. Another design, taken from the T-7 experimental light tank, was selected instead. The T-7 chassis was larger and heavier but still within the overall 18-ton weight limit. The same twin Cadillac V-8 engines and hydromatic transmission used in the M-5 were fitted to the new chassis. They were mounted on rails for quick access and removal.

Armor protection was kept low, from a maximum of 2.5 inches in the turret to a minimum of .9 inch on the hull top, to save weight. But the new light tank's armor was rounded and sloped to achieve greater armor protection than the M-5. In keeping with the theory behind the use of light tanks, the M-24's speed and agility were to make up for what it lost in armor protection.

The new tank was designated the T-24 for testing, which started in October 1943. Initial tests proved so successful that an order for 1,000 was placed immediately. The order was later increased to 5,000. The M-24—as it was designated for oper-

Left: The M-24 Chaffee Light Tank succeeded the M-3 Stuart/M-5 Light Tank in May 1944. **Right:** These American tankers and their M-24 Chaffee guard a strong point near Degu in northwestern Italy.

49

ational purposes—was produced by both Cadillac and Massey-Harris. A total of 4,415 were manufactured before the war ended in 1945. The first M-24s reached American armored units in November 1944 and served throughout the European theater until the end of the war. British forces also received the new M-24, although in nowhere near the numbers of either the M-3 or M-5, and named it after General Adna R. Chaffee, the first commander of the United States armored forces. The United States subsequently adopted the name.

The M-24 saw extensive service in Korea as part of the "combat team" approach, adopted in 1944. In the combat team, one tank design in each category—light, medium, and heavy—was standardized, and its chassis, hull, and power plant served as the basis for the special-purpose vehicles needed to support the tanks in the combat team. The Light Weight combat team included the anti-aircraft tank M-19 Gun, Motor Carriage, which mounted twin 40mm antiaircraft guns, and a self-propelled howitzer—either the M-41 Howitzer Motor Carriage, mounting a 155mm M1 howitzer, or the M-37 Howitzer Motor Carriage, mounting a 105mm M4 howitzer. A recovery vehicle was also intended as part of the team, but it was never produced.

The M-24 was widely used by the United States and other countries, including Great Britain, long after World War II. Even in the late 1980s the M-24 could still be found in operation with a number of smaller nations.

M-24 Chaffee Light Tank	
Country:	United States of America
Type:	Light Tank
Dimensions	
Length:	5.49 m (18 ft)
Width:	2.95 m (9.7 ft)
Height:	2.77 m (9 ft)
Combat weight:	18,207 kg (20 tons)
Engine:	Twin Cadillac 44T24 V-8 220 hp gasoline
Armament:	One 75mm M6 main gun; two .30 caliber Browning machine guns; one .50 caliber Browning machine gun; one M3 mortar
Crew:	5
Speed:	54 km/h (33.5 mph)
Range:	160 km (99 mi)
Obstacle/grade performance:	0.9 m (3 ft)
Date of service:	1944

Left: The M-24 Chaffee was armed with a 75mm main gun and two Browning .30 caliber machine guns. **Right:** The M-24 was named by the British after General Adna R. Chaffee, who was the chief proponent of armored warfare in the United States before the start of WW II.

M-26 General Pershing Heavy Tank

The M-26 Pershing Heavy Tank was the logical result of a program to upgrade the M-4 Sherman Medium Tank. In May 1942 the Ordnance Department received orders to begin development of a new medium tank that would eliminate some of the shortcomings of the M-4. Specifications were established for a new series of experimental tanks designated T-20, T-22, T-23, T-25, and T-26. In general, the specifications called for a tank that would weigh no more than 32 tons, mount an automatic 75 millimeter gun, have frontal armor of at least 4 inches, and be capable of speeds up to 25 miles per hour.

During the next 18 months, the program moved along several lines. Various transmissions, including an electric system designed by General Electric, were tried. The electric system proved too heavy, and a General Motors hydromatic trans-

mission with a torque converter was selected. An auto-loading mechanism was designed and tested, but it proved to be unreliable and was dropped. A new Ford gasoline engine designed specifically for tank use was chosen. The powerful new engine gave the final design a road speed of 30 miles per hour. Torsion bar suspension was selected. The final design was similar to the track system used on the M-24 Chaffee, except that it was driven through a rear sprocket. It had six road wheels and five return wheels.

The design work culminated in the T-26E1 in 1943. However, by this time it was no longer a medium tank. The T-26E1 mounted a 90mm gun, 3.93 inches of armor, and weighed 43.25 tons in its prototype model, 8.5 tons more than the M-4. The T-26E1, redesignated the M-26 General Pershing Heavy Tank in January 1945, was thought to be a match for any-

thing that Germany could throw against it, including the Pz.Kpfw VI Tiger I.

But differences in the theory of armor use among the Ordnance Department, the Armored Force Board—which wanted a fast, heavily gunned tank—and the Army Ground Forces Command (AGFC)—which feared that a tank of those specifications would encourage "tank hunting" when that role was reserved to tank destroyers—delayed serious testing of the new tank. The AGFC was also afraid that the adoption of a heavy tank would cause an already overstrained transatlantic shipping system to further delay armor deliveries. One heavy tank required the shipping space of three medium tanks.

The Ardennes Offensive in December 1944 showed just how poorly matched the M-4 Sherman was against the Ger-

Left: The M-26 Pershing Heavy Tank (with an M-46 Patton to the left) carried a crew of five. **Right:** The M-26, at nearly 42 tons, was the heaviest tank the United States built during WW II.

M-41 Walker Bulldog Light Tank

The M-41 Walker Bulldog (official name: M-41 Combat, Full Tracked: 76MM Gun Walker Bulldog Light Tank) was developed to be a fast and agile light tank for close infantry support and cavalry reconnaissance, yet heavily enough armed to defend itself against medium tanks. Its predecessor was the M-22, which was intended as an air-transportable tank to support airborne troops. Unfortunately, the M-22 was too large for the transport aircraft available during World War II. Similarly, the M-41 ultimately grew so large and heavy that it could not be transported by air in the postwar period. As a consequence, the M-41 found suitable deployment in a limited and counterinsurgency warfare role against lightly armed regular and guerilla troops. Alto-

gether, 1,082 M-41s were built by the Cadillac Division of General Motors at the Cleveland, Ohio, Tank Plant.

The M-41 was named the Walker Bulldog in 1951 to honor General W.W. Walker, who was killed in a jeep accident in Korea that year. It incorporated most of the lessons learned in World War II. It was designed around its engine, a Continental or Lycoming six cylinder, 500 horsepower aircraft engine. The M-41 suspension system used torsion bars and hydraulic shock absorbers. The drive sprocket was at the rear and the idler at the front; there were three return rollers.

The Walker Bulldog carried a 75 millimeter M32 main gun, and one each .30 cali-

ber and .50 caliber Browning machine guns. Its main gun had an automatic loader—the first to ever be used in an American tank. The automatic loader was capable of selecting, lifting, indexing, and ramming, as well as catching and eliminating the empty casings. The main gun also had a bore evacuator to eliminate fumes and an integral fire control system.

The tank was divided into three compartments: front for driving, center for fighting, and rear for the engine. The engine and transmission compartment was separated from the rest of the tank by a fireproof bulkhead. A fire extinguisher system was mounted in the engine compartment. The M-41 was not equipped with a

Left: These M-41 Walker Bulldogs belong to Charlie Company, 82nd Reconnaissance Battalion, 2nd Armored Division. They are participating in Operation Monte Carlo maneuvers held in Western Europe during September 1953.
Right: The M-41 Walker Bulldog was designed and built as a light reconnaissance tank. It entered service in 1950.

close infantry support roles, and even as a tank destroyer. It was deployed in South Vietnam with Republic of Vietnam troops. It also served with Pakistani forces in both wars that nation fought with India and in the Arab–Israeli war of 1967. The M-41 is no longer in service with American forces.

M-41 Walker Bulldog Light Tank	
Country:	United States of America
Type:	Light Tank
Dimensions	
Length:	5.82 m (19 ft)
Width:	3.17 m (10.4 ft)
Height:	2.72 m (8.9 ft)
Combat weight:	23,495 kg (25.9 tons)
Engine:	Continental or Lycoming 6 cylinder air-cooled supercharged 500 hp gasoline
Armament:	One 76mm M32 main gun; one .30 caliber Browning machine gun, coaxial; one .50 caliber Browning machine gun, antiaircraft
Crew:	4
Speed:	72 km/h (44.5 mph)
Range:	160 km (99 mi)
Obstacle/grade performance:	0.71 m (2.3 ft)
Date of service:	1950

nuclear-biological-chemical protection system, but infrared driving and search-lights gave it a night driving and fighting capability.

The M-41 had a crew of four: commander, gunner, loader, and driver. The loader could override the automatic system at any time. The driver sat in the left front of the hull. The other three crewmembers were in the cast-and-welded turret; gunner on the right, loader on the left, and commander behind. The commander and loader each had hatch covers that opened to the rear. The .50 caliber Browning machine gun was mounted near the commander's hatch and used for antiaircraft fire.

The M-41 served as the basis for a series of light armored vehicles. These included the M-41 equipped with a turret designed for the M-551 Sheridan and mounting a 90mm main gun; the M-42 and M-42A1 Duster Antiaircraft vehicle equipped with computer-sighted twin 40mm guns; the M-44 and M-44A1 Special Purpose 155mm Howitzer; the M-52 and M-52A1 Special Purpose 105mm Howitzer; and the M-55 and M-55E1 Special Purpose 203mm Howitzer.

Twenty-four nations purchased the M-41 for their armed forces, including five NATO countries. M-41s were used by New Zealand and Brazil. The M-41 was widely used in Korea in the reconnaissance and

Left: War is 99 percent boredom, as is obvious from the attitude of the commander of this M-41 Walker Bulldog. This tank is hull down in a defensive position near Seoul during the Korean War. **Right:** The M-41 Walker Bulldog saw extensive service during the Korean War and again in South Vietnam. This M-41 belongs to South Vietnamese forces.

M-47 General George S. Patton Medium Tank

The M-47 Patton Medium Tank was an interim design derived from an interim tank. It was developed because the Army needed a medium tank heavier than the M-4 Sherman after the invasion of South Korea by North Korea in 1950.

Following the end of World War II, the majority of the military establishment concerned with the design and use of armor thought that the medium tank concept should be developed further. They had the fine examples of the German Pz.Kpfw V Panther and the Soviet 85 millimeter gunned T-34 to spur them on. Work began to upgrade the M-26 Pershing Heavy Tank to a more heavily armed and gunned medium tank. The result was the M-46 and its slightly up-rated variation, the M-46A1. The M-46 chassis and hull were the same as those used for the M-26, but the new tank had a new engine and transmission built by Continental.

At the same time, development work was also being carried out on a second medium tank concept, designated the T-42. The T-42 was equipped with a new turret mated to a modified T-40 chassis, which in turn was derived from the M-26. The T-40 chassis had been given a new engine and transmission. When the Korean War began in June 1950, the new turret on the T-42 was well along in development but the designers were still working the bugs out of the new chassis. To provide a new medium tank as soon as possible, the T-42 turret with its new 90mm T119 gun was mounted on the M-46 chassis. The result was christened the M-47 Patton.

The M-47's hull was built from cast-and-welded sections. Escape hatches were provided in the floor, rather than through the sides, to secure the hull's integrity. The M-47 was also the last American tank to have a hull machine gunner. He sat on

the right side of the hull to operate his 7.62mm NATO machine gun. The driver sat on the left side of the hull. The gunner sat at the right front of the turret, the loader on the left side, and the commander behind. The loader's station had a rear-opening hatch above. The commander had a separate cupola and rear-opening hatch. Commander and loader stations had periscopes. The gunner also had a periscope as well as a stereoscopic range finder.

The new turret was a massive single-piece casting that provided armor protection nearly 4 inches thick. The rifled 90mm T119 main gun had a sliding block, vertical breech mechanism and used the short recoil, concentric ring mechanism pioneered in the M-24 Light Tank. In the M-47, recoil shock was absorbed by hydraulic compression. One 7.62mm NATO Browning machine gun

Left: The M-47 Medium Tank, here modernized with M-60 components, was one of three tanks to carry the name Patton. The others were the M-46 and the M-48. **Right:** The M-47 Medium Tank and its immediate predecessor, the M-46, were developed from the M-26 Pershing Heavy Tank. The M-47's successor, the M-48, became the first of the American Main Battle Tanks.

tem and warm air heaters for crew comfort. A bulldozer blade kit was developed, and all M-48s had provisions for mounting it on the hull.

The M-48 Patton was the most heavily armored tank in American service to that date. Armor protection ranged from 4.72 inches on the hull's front to 4.3 inches on the turret front down to slightly less than 1 inch on the turret top.

The 90mm M41 main gun used in the M-48 and M-48A1 was equipped with an evacuator, a muzzle brake, and a vertical sliding breech mechanism. The main-gun range finder fed information to the commander's station and the gunner's station. The gunner's ballistic computer was electrically operated but worked on mechanical principles. Solutions to problems were simultaneously fed to gunner and commander. The same ammunition

used in the M-47 was used in the M-48 with only minor variations in muzzle velocity and range.

The M-48 Patton has gone through seven model designations. In 1975 all M-48s of whatever configuration were again modernized to the M-48A5 standard. This modernization included improved armor, an improved fire control system, the 105mm M68 main gun, and a range of other modifications that increased the service life of the M-48 tank. The diesel engine built by Continental was also replaced with an improved model that gave an even greater range. The coaxial machine gun was changed from the 7.62mm Browning 1919A4E1 to the 7.62mm NATO M73 machine gun. A second 7.62mm NATO M73 machine gun was added at the loader's hatch position for antiaircraft use. The commander's hatch also had a machine gun.

The M-48 tank was adopted by at least 19 other nations, including Israel. In fact, the M-48 in various configurations, including variations of Israeli origin, has served with Israeli forces in every war since 1956. No active United States Army units have been equipped with the M-48 Patton since 1984, when the last M-48s were withdrawn from the 2nd Infantry Division in South Korea.

M-48 General George S. Patton Medium Tank (model A5)	
Country:	United States of America
Type:	Medium Tank
Dimensions	
Length:	6.15 mm (20.1 ft)
Width:	3.63 m (11.9 ft)
Height:	3.08 m (10.1 ft)
Combat weight:	45,360 kg (50 tons)
Engine:	Continental AVDS-1790-2D 750 hp diesel
Armament:	One 105mm M68 main gun; three 7.62mm NATO M73 machine guns; one .50 caliber M2 HB machine gun
Crew:	4
Speed:	48 km/h (30 mph)
Range:	499 km (309 mi)
Obstacle/grade performance:	0.9 m (3 ft)
Date of service:	1952

Left: The M-48 Patton during a night firing demonstration.
Right: An M-48A5 Patton guards a convoy during Team Spirit Exercises in South Korea during 1984.

M-60 Main Battle Tank

In 1956 intelligence reports regarding tank development in the Soviet Union suggested that a tank more capable than the T-54/T-55 Main Battle Tank (MBT) was being developed. As the M-48 Medium Tank entered service in 1952, it was considered too heavy, too short-ranged, and too lightly armored to deal with the expected capabilities of the new Soviet tank.

A design team suggested that there was plenty of room for improving the M-48. Upgrade programs were immediately undertaken, beginning with the installation of a new Continental diesel engine. But the ultimate goal, up-gunning to the British L7A1 105 millimeter gun, required a new turret. Authorization was obtained for the new tank design, and the first American MBT entered service in 1960 as the M-60.

Two years later an up-rated M-60, the M-60A1, was put into production. These two versions were followed by 562 M-60A2s, all of which have now been converted to other armored vehicles like the M-60 Armored Vehicle Launched Bridge or the M-728 Combat Engineer Vehicle.

When the capabilities of the new T-62/T-72 MBTs became known in detail, the United States Army began a crash program to up-rate the M-60. The M-60A3 was the result, and it was placed in production in May 1980. More than 15,000 M-60s of various configurations were built before production ended in August 1987.

The M-60 hull is basically the same as that of the M-48. It is built of cast-and-welded sections and divided into three compartments: driving, fighting, and engine/transmission. The new turret is better armored (information concerning the M-60's armor remains classified) and considerably larger, as it has to be to mount the 105mm main gun.

A nuclear-biological-chemical warfare protection system was added in the M-60A3 configuration. It combines over-pressure in the crew compartment with a

Left: A squadron commander belonging to the 1st Battalion, 32nd Armored Regiment, aboard an M-60A3 Main Battle Tank uses hand signals to maneuver his tanks. **Right:** An M-60 fires its 105mm main gun.

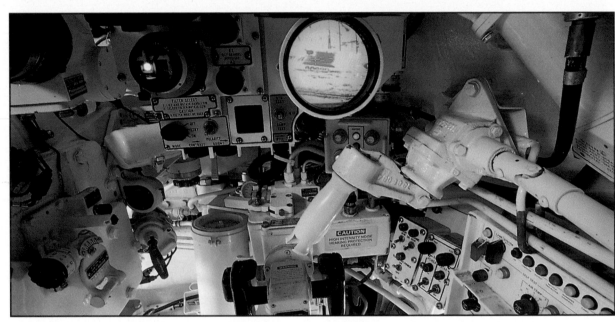

high-capacity central air filtration system. Fresh air is brought directly to each crewmember through a tube. Complete night vision equipment has been fitted to the tank and includes an improved infrared/white light xenon searchlight.

The L7A1 105mm M68 main gun, of British design but built in the United States, is rifled and can fire between six and eight rounds per minute. The tank carries 63 rounds of main gun ammunition, which can be a mix of any of the following: M728 armor-piercing, discarding sabot-tracer; M735 and M735A1 armor-piercing, fin-stabilized, discarding sabot-tracer; M731, with a tungsten penetrator, and M731A, with the stabaloy penetrator;

M774 and M833, both use monobloc stabaloy penetrators; M392A2 armor-piercing, discarding sabot-tracer; M494 anti-personnel-tracer; M456 high-explosive, antitank-tracer; and various target rounds.

The M-60 also carries two machine guns. The commander's cupola is equipped with a .50 caliber M85 antiaircraft machine gun. Mounted coaxially in the hull is the 7.62mm NATO M85, which will be replaced with the M240 machine gun.

The M-60 was up-rated to the A3 configuration beginning in 1977, and the first M-60A3s were sent to Europe and issued to the United States 1st Battalion of the 32nd

Armor Division in 1979. Specific improvements included a new AN/VVG-2 laser range finder connected to an improved fire control system that uses an M21 solid state computer rather than a mechanical one. The new system allows either the gunner or the tank commander to fire the main gun. Bore sighting is made incomparably easier with the laser system.

A new track system with replaceable pads has also been installed in the M-60A3, as well as a newer, more reliable diesel engine. An automatic Halon fire extinguisher system, a smoke-screen system using diesel fuel sprayed into the engine manifold, and the M219 smoke grenade launcher are included. A deep-

Far left: A loader's view of his tank commander. **Left, above:** The gunner's position in the M-60A3 Main Battle Tank. The 105mm main gun's breech is in the left foreground. **Left, below:** The gunner's control unit is located to the far right. The green light indicates the system is functioning properly. **Right:** This M-60A3 carries the M68 105mm main gun. Note the shrouded infrared/white light searchlight above the gun.

delivered to the United States Army on February 28, 1980, and formally named for the late General Creighton W. Abrams, Army Chief of Staff and commander of the 37th Armored Battalion. As a battalion commander, General Abrams had led the armored charge that broke through German siege lines at Bastogne during the Ardennes Offensive in December 1944. The tank was standardized as the M-1 Abrams on February 16, 1981. By the end of production in January 1985, 2,374 M-1 Abrams MBTs had been produced at the Lima and Detroit Arsenal tank plants.

The M-1A1 Abrams evolved from the basic M-1 Abrams. The foremost difference was the mounting of the M256 120mm smoothbore Rheinmetall main gun developed in West Germany. In addition, M-1A1 upgrades involved more armor protection, a new nuclear-biological-chemical protection system that included air-conditioning for the crew, an improved suspension, and a better transmission. The M-1A1 was standardized in Au-

gust 1984, and the first production models were delivered from the Detroit Arsenal in August 1985.

Improvements that were begun in early 1989 added a new commander's station with better weapons handling and a new independent thermal viewer, a carbon dioxide laser range finder, an improved tank-to-tank communication system, new ceramic and reaction-type armor, and a better thermal viewer for the driver.

The Marine Corps has requested the development of a deep-water fording kit and marinization so that the tank will not be affected by saltwater spray or a high-humidity environment. The Marine Corps hopes to replace its fleet of aging M-60 tanks with the M-1A1 Abrams in the 1990s.

M-1 Abrams already fielded in Europe are being replaced with the M-1A1. The returned M-1s are being distributed to the Army Reserve and National Guard until all armored units and prepositioned tank stocks in Europe will have been ex-

changed for the M-1A1. By the end of fiscal year 1988, the 1st and 2nd Armored (Forward) Divisions and the 3rd Infantry Division, all in Europe, plus the 3rd Armored Cavalry Regiment, Fort Bliss, Texas, had received their full allotment of M-1A1s. In the continental United States, the 1st Cavalry, 2nd Armored, 1st Infantry, and 24th Infantry Divisions, and the National Training Center have received the M-1 Abrams, as have National Guard units in North Carolina, South Carolina, Mississippi, and Georgia.

The M-1 Abrams hull and turret are built of a material similar to the ceramic and steel plate Chobham armor developed in Great Britain. The same type of armor is also used on the British Challenger and the West German Leopard 2.

The driver is seated in the middle of the hull in front in a reclining position because of the hull's steep slope. The commander and gunner are in the turret on the right, and the loader is on the left. The fire control system includes a laser range

Left: M-1 Abrams tanks are fielded in Europe as well as with Army Reserve and National Guard units. **Right:** An M-1 Abrams moves carefully through a West German forest during recent exercises.

78

was thicker on Germany's Pz.Kpfw III and IV tanks, but the T-34 could outrange both tanks. To penetrate German armor, the T-34 mounted a 41.2 caliber 76.2mm main gun, capable of penetrating more than 3 inches of armor at 500 yards.

At first the T-34's turret was made of rolled plates welded together. This type of turret was expensive and time-consuming to manufacture, and it was soon replaced with one of cast steel. The T-34 was powered by the same 500 horsepower diesel engine that was used in the BT-7M Fast Tank. The T-34 had a top speed of 31 miles per hour and a range of 186 miles.

Minor changes were made to the T-34 during the course of the war. A new turret configuration with two hatches was designed. The new turret also eliminated an overhang at the rear, a popular place for German infantrymen to slip mines. Armor thickness on the front was increased to nearly 3 inches, and external fuel tanks were added, which increased range to

270 miles. The most significant change, however, occurred in late 1943 after the Battle of Kursk, when a new gun was mounted. The 85mm Model 1934 main gun of 51.5 caliber had been developed specifically to penetrate the armor of the newly deployed German Pz.Kpfw V Panther.

The old 76.2mm gun was barely able to penetrate the thick armor of the Panther and the Tiger I when T-34's were used in massed formations, as they had been at Kursk. But the new gun, adopted from the Model 1939 antiaircraft gun and used on the KV-85 heavy tank, had a muzzle velocity of 2,600 feet per second and could penetrate 3.7 inches of sloped armor at 1,000 yards.

The 85mm gunned T-34 was produced until 1949, when it was replaced by the T-54. The final variant of the T-34 was the T-44, which entered service in the last days of the Great Patriotic War, as World War II is commonly called in the Soviet Union.

The T-44 proved unsatisfactory, and only limited numbers were built. They were used to quell the Hungarian Uprising in 1956.

In all, some 40,000 T-34s and 85mm gunned T-34s were built. They saw service not only with Soviet and Warsaw Pact forces but also with Egypt and Syria in the 1956, 1967, and 1973 Arab–Israeli wars. Copies of the T-34 were built in many Communist Bloc nations, including the People's Republic of China.

T-34 Medium Tank	
Country:	Union of Soviet Socialist Republics
Type:	Fast Tank (Soviet designation)
Dimensions Length: Width: Height:	7.5 m (24.6 ft) 2.9 m (9.5 ft) 2.4 m (7.8 ft)
Combat weight:	25,000 kg (27.5 tons)
Engine:	V-12 water-cooled diesel
Armament:	One main gun, either 76.2mm or 85mm; two 7.62mm DT machine guns
Crew:	**T-34, 76.2mm:** 4 **T-34, 85mm:** 5
Speed:	50 km/h (31 mph)
Range:	300 km (186 mi)
Obstacle/grade performance:	0.8 m (2.6 ft)
Date of service:	1941

Left: The T-34 was supplied to Soviet client forces around the world. An American GI watches a T-34 burn on the road between Inchon and Seoul in South Korea in 1951. **Right:** The T-34 was up-gunned in 1943 with an 85mm main gun. The 85mm gun subsequently became standard on all T-34s, such as this one manufactured in Poland.

T-54/T-55 Main Battle Tank

The T-54/T-55 series of Main Battle Tanks are descended directly from the famous *Prinadlezhit-Chetverki*, or T-34 medium tank, the Soviet Union's armored savior. The T-34 evolved into the T-44 medium tank, which had a different engine, a torsion bar suspension system, a larger chassis, and a dome-shaped turret lying close to the hull.

The T-44 had serious design problems and was not widely produced. Design work on a new, heavier medium tank was started. In 1946 the first prototype of the T-54 rolled onto the testing grounds.

The T-54 was built on the T-44 chassis and had a 100 millimeter Model 1944 main gun. The turret was cast in one piece with the top welded on, a technique Soviet industry worked out for the T-34 turret. Early production models had manual gun-laying systems, but these were later upgraded to powered models. The T-54 carries two 7.62mm machine guns, one in the hull and the other in the turret. A third machine gun is mounted on the turret at the loader's cupola.

The T-54/T-55 fires a wide range of ammunition, including armor-piercing-tracer; high-explosive; armor-piercing, capped-tracer; high-explosive fragmentation; high-explosive, fin-stabilized; and high-velocity, armor-piercing, discarding sabot-tracer.

Left: The T-54, more heavily gunned than the T-34, was supplied to a large number of military forces around the world. This T-54, belonging to the Peruvian Army, is equipped with an infrared searchlight.
Right: The T-44, an unsatisfactory model, became the T-54 when the T-44 chassis was equipped with a new turret and a heavier 100mm main gun.

nance even offers a more powerful main gun in the 105mm L7.

T-54/T-55 Series Medium Tank

Country:	Union of Soviet Socialist Republics
Type:	Main Battle Tank
Dimensions	
Length:	6.4 m (21 ft)
Width:	3.3 m (10.8 ft)
Height:	2.4 m (7.8 ft)
Combat weight:	36,000 kg (39.7 tons)
Engine:	**T-54:** V-12 diesel 520 hp **T-55:** V-12 diesel 580 hp
Armament:	One 100mm D-10T main gun **T-54:** two 7.62mm SGMT machine guns; one 12.7mm DShKm machine gun **T-55:** one 7.62mm SGMT machine gun
Crew:	4
Speed:	**T-54:** 48 km/h (30 mph) **T-55:** 50 km/h (31 mph)
Range:	600 km (372 mi)
Obstacle/grade performance:	0.8 m (2.6 ft)
Date of service:	**T-54:** 1949 **T-55:** 1959 or 1960

Like the T-44, the T-54 uses a torsion bar suspension system. The AV-12 diesel engine is mounted transversely to drive the rear sprockets and produces 520 horsepower. Five rubber-tire road wheels are mounted per side. There are no return wheels; the track runs across the top of the road wheels on its return. The distinguishing identification feature of the T-54/T-55 series is the gap between the first and second road wheels. The T-54 was the first Soviet tank able to operate completely underwater. It can cross rivers at depths down to 18 feet by using a snorkel.

The T-55 model entered service in 1959 or 1960. It is essentially an improved T-54: a more powerful version of the same V-12 diesel engine (580 horsepower), a rotating turret floor, the elimination of the loader's cupola, and an improved transmission. The antiaircraft 12.7mm turret machine gun and the 7.62mm machine gun mounted in the bow plate were removed in the T-55A version to allow more room for main-gun ammunition. The T-55A was given an antiradiation lining, although no version of the T-54 or T-55 has true nuclear-biological-chemical warfare protection for its crew.

The T-54 and T-55 have been built in the Soviet Union, Poland, Czechoslovakia, and the People's Republic of China. Estimates of total numbers vary from 42,000 to 57,000. The T-55 is still in wide use with Soviet and Warsaw Pact forces—estimates range between 31,000 and 39,000. The series is, or has been, used in some 47 other nations on both sides of the Iron Curtain. The T-54/T-55 series has proved so popular that a British company offers a complete rebuild package to modernize them with a more powerful Rolls Royce diesel, a modern fire control system, and a modern suspension system. Royal Ord-

Left: The T-55 was basically the T-54 with a new turret and more powerful engine. This T-55 was knocked out by South Vietnamese antitank gunners near An Loc. **Right:** The United States has acquired a number of Soviet tanks as a result of the wars in the Middle East. This American-owned Soviet T-54 is used to simulate oppositional forces during military training.

The T-62's main gun is the 115mm U-5TS smoothbore. Because of the length of the shell, the main gun elevates after each recoil. This, coupled with the complicated fire control system, means the tank can maintain a rate of only four to five rounds per minute. Also, the turret cannot be traversed during the loading sequence. This combination of drawbacks made the T-62 particularly vulnerable to Israeli tanks during the 1973 Yom Kippur War and the 1982 invasion of Lebanon. Only 40 rounds of main-gun ammunition can be carried. One 7.62mm PKT ma-

chine gun is located coaxially with the main gun, and a 12.7mm DShKM machine gun is mounted on the turret for antiaircraft use.

The T-62 and T-62A—larger, differently contoured turret, no loader's hatch, and an externally mounted 12.7mm DShKM machine gun—have been updated with a laser range finder, a solid state ballistic computer, new infrared driving and searchlights, and an image intensifier for night work. The T-62M version has been fitted with the same track used on the T-

72. Appliqué and reaction armor have also been installed on some T-62s. The British company Royal Ordnance manufactures a copy of the 115mm gun barrel for use by Egypt.

The T-62 is in use by some 23 countries, including Iran and Iraq, who both fielded it during their 1980–88 war. The United States obtained T-62s from Israel and Egypt and uses them at the National Training Center. Israel also uses the T-62; their supply was captured from Arab antagonists.

T-62 Main Battle Tank	
Country:	Union of Soviet Socialist Republics
Type:	Main Battle Tank
Dimensions	
Length:	6.63 m (21.7 ft)
Width:	3.3 m (10.8 ft)
Height:	2.39 m (7.8 ft)
Combat weight:	40,000 kg (44 tons)
Engine:	Model 55 V-12 diesel 580 hp
Armament:	One 115mm U-5TS smoothbore main gun; one 7.62mm PKT machine gun; one 12.7mm DShkm machine gun
Crew:	4
Speed:	50 km/h (31 mph)
Range:	450 km (279 mi)
Obstacle/grade performance:	0.8 m (2.6 ft)
Date of service:	1961

Left: A potential confrontation of the future as a result of the Cold War: American A-10 Warthog attack jets swoop over a Soviet T-62 tank. **Right:** The T-62 has seen extensive service in the Middle East with Syrian and Egyptian forces during the 1960s, '70s, and '80s, but it proved no match for Israeli Merkavas during the 1982 invasion of Lebanon.

T-64 Main Battle Tank

The T-64 Main Battle Tank (MBT) was known as the T-72 to Western intelligence agencies for several years, even before the public advent of the T-62. Then in 1977 a new Soviet tank was identified, and the confusion began. At first, it was thought the new tank was a variant of the older model. But then, as more information and clearer photographs were obtained, the differences became obvious. The old-model tank had six small dual road wheels that were made by a stamping process; the new tank had six large, die-cast dual road wheels with three return rollers. This last element had not been seen on Soviet tanks since the World War II KV and JS series of heavy tanks. In addition, while both tanks had automatic loaders, the new model tank's auto-loading mechanism was of a different type. The old model tank was reclassified by NATO as the T-64, the new model was called the T-72.

The T-64's hull is divided into three compartments: driving in the front, fighting in the center, and the engine in the rear. The crewmembers are arranged in the T-64 in a slightly different manner than is usual in Soviet tanks. The driver remains in the front of the hull in the center. However, since the T-64 uses an auto-loading mechanism for the main gun, the commander and gunner are seated differently in the turret, the commander to the right, the gunner to the left. The auto-loading mechanism eliminates the need for a loader.

The T-64 has a hydraulic-mechanical suspension system rather than the usual torsion bar suspension, and it is powered by a five-cylinder diesel engine. In addition to the differences between the T-72 and the T-64 noted above, the T-64 has a slightly smaller turret. The infrared/white light searchlight is on the left side of the main gun rather than the right, as with the T-72, and two or three rectangular ammunition boxes are mounted on the left side of the turret. These boxes hold ammunition belts for the 12.7mm DShKM machine gun mounted ahead of the commander's cupola. The T-64 almost always carries its long snorkel tube fastened to a rack on the turret bustle when in the field.

The T-64A (NATO designation) or T-64 M1981/1 (Soviet designation) has a modified gun sight, smoke mortars on the front of the turret, and side skirt armor attaching to points along the fenders. The T-64B is equipped to fire the AT8 Songster antitank guided missile. The main gun is a 125 millimeter smoothbore. The gun is fed from a dual carousel auto-loader located on the hull floor that picks up both shell and powder charge. The gun is stabilized so the tank can shoot accurately while moving. Rate of fire is five to eight rounds per minute, but there have been doubts cast on the reliability of the auto-loading mechanism.

T-64 production came to an end in 1981. At the end of 1988, the T-64 was in service only with Soviet troops inside the Soviet Union and units assigned to Soviet forces in East Germany. It is the MBT found in the 2nd Guards Army, the 3rd Shock Army, and the 20th Guards Army. T-64s have also been observed with the Southern Group of Soviet forces in Hungary. American intelligence sources think that the T-64 was not as satisfactory a design as the Soviets had wished. Evidence for this is the tank's low production, as well as its lack of distribution among Warsaw Pact forces or Soviet client states in the Middle East, Africa, or Latin America.

T-64 Main Battle Tank			
Country:	Union of Soviet Socialist Republics	**Armament:**	One 125mm 2A46 smoothbore main gun; one 7.62mm PKT machine gun; one 12.7mm DShKM machine gun
Type:	Main Battle Tank		
Dimensions		**Crew:**	3
Length:	6.4 m (21 ft)		
Width:	3.8 m (12.4 ft)		
Height:	2.3 m (7.5 ft)		
		Speed:	70 km/h (43 mph)
Combat weight:	38,000 kg (41.9 tons)	**Range:**	450 km (279 mi)
Engine:	Five cylinder diesel 700 to 750 hp	**Obstacle/grade performance:**	0.91 m (3 ft)
		Date of service:	1970

Right: The T-64 Main Battle Tank is the predecessor to the T-72, the Soviet Union's most widely deployed MBT. The T-64 MBT was not a satisfactory design, and it has not been provided to Soviet client forces.

T-72 Main Battle Tank

The T-72 Main Battle Tank (MBT) is thought to have entered production at State Factory Number 183—the Nizhni-Tagil Railroad Enterprise—in 1972. Hints and rumors of its existence circulated until it was observed at close hand by the French Minister of Defense in 1977. At first it was thought to be a variation of the T-64, but it is now known to have been a comprehensive redesign.

The T-72 is quite heavily armored. Protection ranges from 11 inches on the turret face to 8.8 inches of spaced, laminate armor on the hull nose, which is inclined so as to provide the equivalent of 21.5 inches of armor. The T-72 is fitted with rectangular side armor plates that cover the vulnerable hydraulic shock absorbers at a 60° angle. When the plates are unclipped, they spring out to the 60° inclination. The tank also has a protective, full-length skirt.

A bulldozer blade is mounted on the T-72's nose and can be deployed to dig firing positions or clear debris. An infrared searchlight is mounted on the right side of the main gun, just the opposite of the T-64. The T-72 carries a snorkel clipped to the left side of the turret. The T-72 uses the torsion bar suspension system, which is usual for Soviet MBTs. Western intelligence sources consider it superior to the hydraulic-mechanical system used on the T-64. The T-72 has six road wheels per side that are quite a bit bigger than those used on the T-64. Three return rollers are used to guide the track on its return. Like the T-64, the T-72 is driven through the rear sprocket.

A 7.62 millimeter PKT machine gun is mounted in the turret coaxially with the main gun and can be fired automatically. A 12.7mm DShKM machine gun is mounted ahead of the hatch on the commander's cupola, but it can be fired only with the hatch open and the commander standing halfway out. This makes him an obvious target for snipers. The main gun

is the same 125mm smoothbore Model 2A46 that is used on the T-64. It is fed from an automatic carousel loader mounted on the hull floor. Ammunition capacity is 39 rounds. The T-72 fires armor-piercing, fin-stabilized, discarding sabot (APFSDS) rounds at a velocity of 5,298 feet per second, which can penetrate nearly 12 inches of armor at 1,100 yards; high-explosive, antitank, fin-stabilized (HEAT-FS) at 2,952 feet per second, which can penetrate nearly 19 inches of armor at 1,100 yards; and high-explosive, fragmentation rounds (HE-FRAG) at 2,788 feet per second. The usual mix, based on captured Syrian T-72s, is thought to be 12 APFSDS, 21 HE-FRAG, and six HEAT-FS per carousel. The ammunition in the carousel is contained on two levels, powder charge below, projectile above. As with the T-64, the main gun is stabilized, allowing the T-72 to shoot while moving on the road or cross-country.

The T-72 has full nuclear-biological-chemical protection. The interior of the tank is also lined with a lead-impregnated material for protection against radiation and neutron pulses.

During the 1982 invasion of Lebanon, the Israeli Army, using the Merkava's 105mm main gun and TOW antitank missiles, was able to destroy a large number of T-72s operated by Syrian armored forces. Since then, the Soviets have conducted an extensive upgrade program in order to improve the tank's armor and survivability. Appliqué armor, fender skirts, and reaction armor boxes have all been added.

The United States Department of Defense estimates that more than 17,000 T-72 tanks have been built at four tank production facilities in the Soviet Union. Several variations of the T-72 are known, but the changes are minor. The only exception is the T-72 M1981/3, which is called the T-80 in the West. The T-72 has been distributed to 15 nations in Eastern Eu-

rope, the Middle East, and Africa. It is manufactured in Czechoslovakia, India, Poland, and Yugoslavia. The T-72 is the numerical mainstay of Soviet MBT forces in Eastern Europe.

T-72 Main Battle Tank

Country:	Union of Soviet Socialist Republics
Type:	Main Battle Tank
Dimensions	
Length:	6.9 m (22.6 ft)
Width:	3.6 m (11.8 ft)
Height:	2.37 m (7.7 ft)
Combat weight:	41,000 kg (45.2 tons)
Engine:	12 cylinder diesel 780 hp multifuel
Armament:	One 125mm 2A465 smoothbore main gun; one 7.62mm PKT machine gun; one 12.7mm DShKM machine gun
Crew:	3
Speed:	60 km/h (37 mph)
Range:	480 km (298 mi)
Obstacle/grade performance:	0.9 m (3.0 ft)
Date of service:	1977

Right: The T-72 Main Battle Tank is a more sophisticated version of the earlier T-64. It is powered by a 12 cylinder engine capable of burning a variety of fuels. **Far right:** The Soviet T-72 entered production in 1972. It carries a powerful 125mm smoothbore main gun that fires a wide variety of fin-stabilized rounds.

Officially, NATO forces call it the FST, which stands for Future Soviet Tank or Follow-on Soviet Tank. Unofficially, the two versions under development are being called the Soviet T-2000 series of tanks.

At present, the Soviets continue to develop new tank technology with great speed. Under development are two new designs that are being called the FST-1 and FST-2. The FST-1 is believed to be a second-generation T-80 Main Battle Tank (MBT) that will sport heavier armor, a new lower-profile turret, and a more powerful 135 millimeter gun. The FST-1 tank will have its reactive armor protection integrated into the tank's hull rather than bolted on, as with the T-80. Designers reduced the size of the conventional turret, and it is now believed the new tank may tip the scales at 35 to 37 tons. The Soviets are believed to have built approximately 125 FST-1 tanks to date, and all are undergoing extensive tests and evaluation.

As they struggle to counter the proliferation of NATO antitank missiles and rockets, the Soviets are also believed to be developing a revolutionary tank design called the FST-2. At present, it is believed that if the Soviets give the FST-2 high priority in terms of development, the turretless tank with its electrothermal or electromagnetic cannon could be fielded by the mid-1990s. The FST-2 will likely become the Soviet MBT by the beginning of the 21st century.

The FST-2 will be armed with an electrothermal fire control system. Projectiles would be propelled much farther and faster than conventional powder-charged munitions. The system works by pumping gases into the breech of the cannon and then igniting them with an electrical charge through a controlled explosion. A conventional tank round travels at 3,000 to 3,500 feet per second. The FST-2 may be capable of firing rounds from its 140mm to 145mm cannon

at speeds up to 6,000 feet per second. This not only would make the projectile the largest in use on an MBT but also far more powerful and long-ranging than anything in any other nation's inventory. If the Soviets develop an electromagnetic system, a series of precise magnets would be used to fire a nonexplosive projectile at velocities between 10,000 and 12,000 feet per second.

The FST-2 is believed to have a crew of two, will sport an automatic loading cannon for its 40-round capacity, and have a range of more than 300 miles. Of even greater concern to many military experts is the possibility that the FST-2 may have an electrically charged "protective" armor system. Unlike conventional reactive armor tiles, which have to be struck with a projectile to cause the armor tile to explode and thus blunt the antitank round's effect, electronic armor may be the closest thing to an actual force field to yet be incorporated onto a combat vehicle. As a tank-killing round nears the FST-2, the electronic field around the tank is penetrated, completing the circuit. Instantly, a powerful electric charge closes the electric barrier, and the missile becomes so electrically charged that it literally destroys itself. The key to such new technology is generating the large amounts of electricity needed to power the force field and the electromagnetic or electrothermal cannon within the confines of a tank-size vehicle. If the Soviets use capacitors to store the energy rather than trying to generate it, the possibilities of success are well within reach.

The evolutionary FST-1 would likely be the interim tank while the more revolutionary FST-2 is field-tested and readied for production.

FST-1 and 2			
Country:	Union of Soviet Socialist Republics	Armament:	machine gun **FST-2:** One 140mm to 145mm electromagnetic main gun; two 7.62mm machine guns
Type:	Main Battle Tank		
Dimensions		Crew:	2 or 3
Length:	7.5 m (26.4 ft)(approximate)		
Width:	3.4 m (11.2 ft)(approximate)	Speed:	80 km/h (50 mph) (approximate)
Height:	**FST-1:** 2.1 m (6.9 ft) (approximate) **FST-2:** 2 m (6.5 ft)		
Combat weight:	**FST-1:** 31,750 to 33,500 kg (35 to 37 tons) **FST-2:** 31,750 kg (35 tons)	Range:	400 km (248 mi) (approximate)
		Obstacle/grade performance:	**FST-1:** 0.9 m (2.95 ft) **FST-2:** 0.9 to 1.3 m (3 to 4.2 ft) (approximate)
Engine:	**FST-1:** Gas turbine 985 hp **FST-2:** Unknown		
		Date of service:	**FST-1:** 1991 (approximate) **FST-2:** 1995 to 1997 (approximate)
Armament:	**FST-1:** One 135mm smoothbore main gun; one 7.62mm		

Right: The Future Soviet Tank (NATO designation FST-1 and FST-2) is now being developed in the Soviet Union. This sketch shows a heavily armored tank with a low silhouette and a 135mm main gun mounted in the hull.

Panzerkampfwagens I and II

What had been referred to in all official documents as "agricultural tractors" to disguise their true nature were, in fact, military tanks. But it was not until 1935 that the new Nazi government, which had approved their acquisition, was ready to defy the Versailles Treaty of 1919 (which limited the German armed forces to 100,000 men and no tanks or fighter aircraft) and admit the true nature of the tanks. In the meantime, these two new tanks of the arrogant Third Reich were intended for use as training vehicles for the new armored division concept developed by General Heinz Guderian, the Chief of Staff to the Inspectorate of Motorized Troops.

But building modern tanks virtually from scratch proved far tougher and more time-consuming than anyone had anticipated—especially with Adolf Hitler constantly changing priorities. The two new tanks, designated Panzerkampfwagen (Pz.Kpfw) I and II (military designations, SdKfz 101 and SdKfz 121), were drafted as war weapons. They formed the armored force that broke the Polish Army in three weeks during September 1939. Nine months later, they were still the armored core of the *blitzkrieg* that smashed the mightiest fighting force in Europe, the French Army.

In the early days of the Third Reich, Guderian correctly perceived that Hitler was hell-bent on unleashing war on the European continent to avenge the German defeat in 1918 and the dishonorable peace (as perceived by Germany) that had been imposed. Influenced by the writings of Charles de Gaulle, France's preeminent military tactician who was ignored by the French military establishment, and England's Basil Liddell Hart, Guderian strove all through the 1930s to build the new Panzer divisions—a combination of tanks, infantry in motor vehicles, motor-drawn artillery, scouting troops on motorcycles, and necessary support units. The first of the new Panzer divisions

was formed in 1935, and their tanks were the Pz.Kpfw I and II.

The Pz.Kpfw I was designed to a general specification set by the new Nazi government. They were produced by industrial giant Krupp Werke, which won a design runoff. The chassis was based on the British Carden-Loyd tankette. A 57 horsepower Krupp gasoline engine drove the front sprockets. The tank weighed not quite six tons in the original version. It mounted a hand-cranked turret in which the commander stood—the driver sat below in the hull—and two 7.92 millimeter machine guns were mounted for the commander's use. Armor plating between .25 and .5 inch thick protected the crew against small arms fire. Capable of traveling up to 125 miles at a top speed of 23 miles per hour, the Pz.Kpfw I could cross vertical obstacles more than 14 inches high and span four-foot trenches.

Production began in 1934, and trials that year showed that the Pz.Kpfw I was badly underpowered. A new, more powerful Maybach 100 horsepower engine was in-

stalled, which required that the chassis be lengthened by 17 inches. This in turn required a fifth road, or bogie, wheel.

Pz.Kpfw II was a stopgap measure meant to provide the German Army with a medium-weight training tank until Guderian could find sufficient backing to bring the Pz.Kpfw III and IV, his fighting tanks, into production. But the Pz.Kpfw II, in partnership with the Pz.Kpfw I, was destined to spearhead the *blitzkrieg* into Poland and France because they were the only tanks Germany had in 1939. Thousands of Pz.Kpfw IIs were also thrown against Russia in 1941.

Even though the Pz.Kpfw II was intended as a trainer, it was designed to fight other tanks. It carried relatively thick armor for its time: a maximum of 1.2 inches on the hull nose and slightly less on the turret face in the original Ausf A model. It was equipped with a 30 caliber 20mm gun and one 7.92mm machine gun. At the time production began, the 20mm gun could penetrate 1 inch of armor at 500 yards, enough to defeat any tank.

Left: The German Pz.Kpfw I light tank was originally intended as a training tank. It was armed only with two machine guns. **Right:** Pz.Kpfw I specifications were issued as early as 1932. It was designated as an agricultural tractor to disguise its true purpose. **Far right:** The Pz.Kpfw II medium tank was also designed and built as a training tank. It carried a 20mm main gun.

provided more protection but took nearly ten miles per hour off the tank's speed. Nevertheless, nearly 1,100 Pz.Kpfw II Ausf A, B, C, F, J, and Ks participated in the invasion of Russia in June 1941.

Again, superior tactics rather than equipment enabled the German Army to push deep into Russia on three fronts. Within five months, Moscow, more than 1,500 miles from the invasion's jump-off point, was under siege. But with the introduction of new Soviet tanks—notably the T-34—the Pz.Kpfw II was no longer a viable design. The numbers tell the story. Of the nearly 1,100 Pz.Kpfw IIs that began the invasion, less than 870 were still in service ten months later, despite intensive production to make up battle losses. Increasingly after 1942 the Pz.Kpfw II was relegated to other roles, most notably as a self-propelled weapon mounting a variety of guns, from the PaK 40/2 75mm to a 105mm howitzer. Known as *Panzerjägers*, this series of tank destroyers was issued to armored and infantry units. Thus the Pz.Kpfw II was the only tank in the German armed forces to serve as a tank through the entire war.

Panzerkampfwagen I (SdKfz 101) Light Tank

Country:	Germany
Type:	Light Tank, training (originally)
Dimensions	
Length:	4.03 m (13.2 ft)
Width:	2.05 m (6.7 ft)
Height:	1.71 m (5.6 ft)
Combat weight:	5,046 kg (5.6 tons)
Engine:	Krupp M305 gasoline 60 hp
Armament:	Two 7.92mm Model 1934 machine guns
Crew:	2
Speed:	37 km/h (23 mph)
Range:	200 km (124 mi)
Obstacle/grade performance:	0.41 m (1.3 ft)
Date of service:	1934

Panzerkampfwagen II (SdKfz 121) Medium Tank

Country:	Germany
Type:	Medium Tank
Dimensions	
Length:	4.81 m (15.8 ft)
Width:	2.28 m (7.5 ft)
Height:	2.02 m (6.6 ft)
Combat weight:	8,436 kg (9.3 tons)
Engine:	Maybach HL 62 gasoline
Armament:	One KwK 20mm 30 caliber gun; one 7.92mm Model 1934 machine gun
Crew:	3
Speed:	40 km/h (25 mph)
Range:	190 km (118 mi)
Obstacle/grade performance:	0.42 m (1.4 ft)
Date of service:	1935

Left: The Panzer II medium tank, shown here being loaded aboard special transporters, weighed only about nine tons. **Right:** In this rare photograph, a Pz.Kpfw 38(T) can be seen moving in advance of a Pz.Kpfw II during the invasion of France in May and June 1940. The Pz.Kpfw 38(T) was originally known as the CKD/Praga TNHP and was designed and built in Czechoslovakia.

Panzerkampfwagens III and IV

General Heinz Guderian, building on experience gained in the design of the Pz.Kpfw I, pushed hard for the mainstay of his Panzer divisions, a new 15-ton light tank—the Pz.Kpfw III (military designation, SdKfz 141). Production began in 1936, but manufacturing went slowly as Guderian fought the army's bureaucracy, the Nazi government's shifting priorities, and a shortage of raw materials and design experience. A number of prototype vehicles were tested before the design was standardized in September 1938. By December 1939 only 157 Pz.Kpfw IIIs had been built.

The Pz.Kpfw III was not a major advance in tank development. Rather, it was specific to the tactics Guderian had in mind. It had a high-velocity gun (the 45 caliber 37 millimeter antitank gun used by the infantry), a crew of five so that each member would not be overwhelmed by a multitude of tasks when under fire, a radio and intercom system, a ten-speed transmission, and a vastly improved suspension and road wheel system. To keep weight within reasonable bounds, armor was kept at the same thickness as that used in the early models of the Pz.Kpfw II. In the matter of main armament, Guderian was forced to compromise. He had wanted a 50mm high-velocity gun, but Ordnance insisted on the 37mm infantry antitank gun in the interests of standardization. However, the turret ring was made large enough so the tank could be up-gunned at a later date.

The interior design of the Pz.Kpfw III was exceptionally well thought out—as it had to be for a crew of five. The tank commander and gunner sat in the revolving turret compartment. The driver sat forward on the left side in the main hull, the radio operator to the rear. The loader had sufficient room to stand and move the heavy shells from storage bins to gun.

Only a small number of Pz.Kpfw IIIs took part in the invasion of Poland in the fall of 1939. But on May 8, 1940, most of the 349 Pz.Kpfw IIIs that had been built were operating in the XIX Panzer Corps, which was responsible for the breakthrough in the Ardennes region. The minimal armor and 37mm gun were no match for the French Char B Heavy Tank or the S-35 Medium Tank on a one-to-one basis, but concentration of forces and superior tactics enabled the Germans to run right over Allied tanks operating in support of infantry. At one point, General Erwin Rommel was able to move his armored forces 175 miles in one day, a record that still stands.

Experimentation and modification continued, and the Pz.Kpfw IIIs that invaded Russia and served in North Africa were more powerful and capable than the original Pz.Kpfw III. After the fall of France, Hitler ordered the 50mm antitank gun mounted on all Pz.Kpfw IIIs. At the same time, he stood German industry

Left: A Pz.Kpfw IV drives through a ruined Belgian town on June 17, 1944. The Pz.Kpfw IV Ausf D shown here carried a 24 caliber 75mm gun. **Right:** The Pz.Kpfw III was the first tank built by the Nazi government that was designed for actual combat. The task of the Pz.Kpfw III was to take on and defeat enemy tanks. It was originally armed with a high-velocity 45 caliber 37mm gun. Later models (Ausf F and on) were armed with a more powerful 50mm gun.

The Pz.Kpfw IV Ausf F, or F model, was armed with a short-barrel 75mm gun (combat experience in France highlighted the shortcomings of the original 50mm), was driven by a 250 horsepower Maybach engine (later up-rated to 300 horsepower), and had a top speed of 26 miles per hour. Armor plate on the Pz.Kpfw IV was very thin—varying from .75 inch to a little more than 1 inch on the turret and hull front. In upgrade programs appliqué armor brought total protection up to 2.3 inches in later models. The interior layout was the same as for the Pz.Kpfw III.

Nearly 280 Pz.Kpfw IVs were distributed throughout the ten Panzer divisions that took part in the invasion of France in May and June of 1940. Hitler stood wartime production down in July of that year, and as a result, there were only 580 Pz.Kpfw IVs available to the Panzer divisions that invaded Russia in June 1941. The Pz.Kpfw IV served on every front and was heavily engaged against Soviet tanks. Until the T-34 and the KV-1 entered Soviet service, the Pz.Kpfw IV was the boss of the battlefield.

When it became apparent that the Pz.Kpfw IV was the only German tank that could be up-gunned to meet the Soviet KV-1s and T-34s as equals, Hitler ordered priority production. A new gun, the KwK 40 75mm L/48, and a larger turret were mounted on the Ausf G model in 1943. With this gun, the Pz.Kpfw IV proved the equal of the Soviet T-34 and KV-1. It was also very effective against the range of British tanks and the American M-4 Sherman. It operated successfully in Russia, Western Europe, the Balkans, North Africa, and Italy. Over 8,000 Pz.Kpfw IVs were built before Nazi Germany collapsed in May 1945; it was the only German tank to stay in continuous production during the entire war. The Pz.Kpfw IV last saw action during the 1967 Arab–Israeli War in the hands of Syrian tankers.

Panzerkampfwagen III (SdKfz 141) Light Tank	
Country:	Germany
Type:	Light Tank
Dimensions	
Length:	5.41 m (17.75 ft)
Width:	2.92 m (9.6 ft)
Height:	2.51 m (8.2 ft)
Combat weight:	18,144 kg (20 tons)
Engine:	Maybach HL V-12 gasoline
Armament:	One KwK 50mm gun; two 7.92mm Model 1934 machine guns
Crew:	5
Speed:	40 km/h (25 mph)
Range:	175 km (109 mi)
Obstacle/grade performance:	0.6 (2 ft)
Date of service:	1936

Panzerkampfwagen IV (SdKfz 161) Medium Tank	
Country:	Germany
Type:	Medium Tank
Dimensions	
Length:	5.91 m (19.4 ft)
Width:	2.92 m (9.6 ft)
Height:	2.59 m (8.5 ft)
Combat weight:	19,700 kg (21.7 tons)
Engine:	Maybach HL 120 V-12 gasoline
Armament:	One KwK 75mm gun; two 7.92mm Model 1934 coaxial machine guns
Crew:	5
Speed:	40 km/h (25 mph)
Range:	190 km (200 mi)
Obstacle/grade performance:	0.6 m (2 ft)
Date of service:	1936

Left: This Pz.Kpfw IV Ausf H has been fitted with side plates surrounding the turret on three sides, as well as on either side of the hull. The hull plates were quite thin and protected the crew from rifle fire only. **Right:** The Pz.Kpfw IV served in every major engagement on all fronts. More than 8,000 tanks were produced before the war ended. **Far right:** The Pz.Kpfw IV Ausf E with nose armor plating removed. Note the appliqué armor plates around the turret.

thrown into battle as a "stiffener" to back up the Pz.Kpfw III and IV combinations. But at their Leningrad and Kursk debuts in late 1942 and July 1943 respectively, Tiger I tanks were sent into battle in small, unsupported units after inadequate planning. They were too few and spread too far apart as they attacked Soviet antitank defenses of greater depth than had ever been seen before. Nearly all of these Tigers were destroyed.

But as the German Army learned to use the Tiger I to its best advantage, its reputation grew to awesome and legendary proportions. Its heavy armor made it practically impervious to frontal attack, and its high-velocity 88mm gun was ready to chastise anything that came within range. The Tiger I's main gun could knock out a T-34 tank at a distance greater than three miles. In July 1944 one

Tiger I destroyed 25 tanks of the British Seventh Armored Division—Desert Rats—before it was finally knocked out from behind. In fact, attack from behind was the only effective way Allied tanks could deal with the Tiger I. Using superior mobility, Allied tanks had to maneuver for an attack from behind or from the side if they had any hope at all of taking a Tiger I down. The Tiger I's turret traversed very slowly, requiring 15 seconds for a 360° turn. And if the drive motor went down, 750 turns of a hand crank were needed to accomplish the same turn.

Other major drawbacks to the Tiger were its limited range, 62 miles, and low speed, 24 miles per hour. The Tiger I had eight overlapping road wheels on each side in a staggered pattern (some toward the inside of the tank, some toward the outside). Snow and ice could become

packed in the treads and wheels and freeze overnight in the cold Russian winters. The Soviets quickly learned to attack at dawn, when the Tiger's tracks were frozen solid.

Despite its heavy armor and main gun, the Tiger I was phased out of production in August 1944 after a production run of about 1,300. Even so, it saw service on every front from North Africa to the eastern front.

Panzerkampfwagen VI (SdKfz 181) Tiger I	
Country:	Germany
Type:	Heavy Tank
Dimensions	
Length:	8.25 m (27 ft)
Width:	3.73 m (12.2 ft)
Height:	2.85 m (9.3 ft)
Combat weight:	55,000 kg (60.6 tons)
Engine:	Maybach HL 230 V-12 gasoline
Armament:	One KwK 36 88mm L/56 main gun; two 7.92mm Model 1934 machine guns
Crew:	5
Speed:	38 km/h (24 mph)
Range:	100 km (62 mi)
Obstacle/grade performance:	0.8 m (2.6 ft)
Date of service:	1942

Left: This view of the Tiger I shows the interleaved road wheels coated with mud. The wheels could easily jam if the mud froze—as it often did on the eastern front. **Right:** This Tiger I, found at Haustenbeck, Germany, was shipped to England after the war. **Right, top:** The Tiger I was a major departure in German tank design. The army needed a tank that could outgun the Soviet T-34 and KV-1 and penetrate the armor on British tanks. They achieved it by arming the Tiger I with their 88mm antiaircraft gun.

Panzerkampfwagen V Panther

Following the fall of Kiev in September 1941, an offensive in the direction of Orel was begun by the II Panzer Army on September 30, 1941. The 4th Panzer Division was part of the II Panzer Army, and on October 6 it was pushing hard on the Russian town of Mzensk when it was attacked on its flank and badly shot up. The Soviet T-34 tank had made its first appearance in the war. In his diary, German General Heinz Guderian noted, "This was the first occasion on which the apparent superiority of the Russian T-34 to our tanks became plainly apparent . . . the rapid advance on Tula which we had planned had therefore to be abandoned for the moment."

The appearance of the T-34 galvanized the General Staff and German military planners as few other incidents had done. The Chancellery granted almost immediate priority, and by January 1942 detailed specifications had been drawn up for a new medium tank armed with a heavy gun, yet fast enough to deal with the new Soviet T-34, as well as the KV-1 heavy tank, which had also made an appearance. By April, designs were finalized and the first production tanks appeared.

Dubbed the Pz.Kpfw V Panther (military designation, SdKfz 171), its hull construction was little different from the Pz.Kpfw IV, except in size. It was given a well-sloped turret and massive mantlet (armor surrounding the barrel of the main gun where it leaves the turret) through which the long-barrel 75 millimeter gun protruded. The new tank was powered by a Maybach 700 horsepower gasoline engine and had a range of 110 miles. Frontal armor was nearly 5 inches thick. The long gun fired an armor-piercing shell at a velocity of 3,068 feet per second, and it could penetrate 4.75 inches of armor plate sloped 30° from a distance of 1,094 yards. The Panther could knock out any tank in the Allied inventory until almost the end of the war, including the Soviet T-34, KV-1, and JS-1 tanks.

Left: The 45-ton Panther medium tank was built by Germany to counter the Soviet T-34 medium tank. **Right:** U.S. Army troops examine a Pz.Kpfw V Panther Ausf D that was knocked out of action in Italy. The tank is coated with Zimmeritt antimagnetic paste, which prevents mines and satchel charges from being attached to the tank's hull by magnets.

Leopard 1 Main Battle Tank

In 1955, ten years after the end of World War II, the Federal Republic of Germany was allowed to rearm and was invited to join the North Atlantic Treaty Organization (NATO). In 1957 Germany and France, and later Italy, agreed to cooperate in designing and building a new Main Battle Tank (MBT). Two design teams were formed in Germany and one in France. The first prototypes, both from German teams, were ready for testing in 1960. In 1962 trials between the French design, the AMX-30, and German tank prototypes were conducted. The following year the German government decided that the *Standardpanzer* design, now known as the Leopard, was more suitable

for its needs. Thus, the design partnership ended. France sent the AMX-30 into production. Italy first thought to design and build its own MBT, but then decided to buy the American M-60 MBT as a replacement for its M-47 medium tanks.

Given Germany's history of successful tank production and use, it would seem logical that the Leopard would be an extension of the technology developed for the Panther and Tiger series of tanks. In fact, it is not. Following Germany's unconditional surrender in May 1945, the Allies made certain that all military production facilities were completely dismantled. So the Germans had to begin from scratch

when they designed and built the Leopard tank.

The Leopard 1 is a modern MBT of 1960s derivation. It is heavily gunned and armored, although less so than the Soviet MBTs it was designed to face. The Leopard 1 has a conventional hull divided by a fireproof bulkhead into an engine compartment aft and a crew compartment forward. The entire turret is cast in one piece. The commander and gunner are in the turret on the right. The loader is on the left in the turret and hefts shells into the main gun's breech, which opens and ejects the empty shell on recoil. The driver is in the front of the hull on the right-

Left: This West German Army Leopard 1 has been fitted with a SIMFIRE practice system, which permits the tank crew to simulate main-gun fire. **Right:** The Leopard 1, shown here during recent Operation Reforger exercises in West Germany, is also used by the armies of Australia, Belgium, Canada, Greece, Italy, Libya, the Netherlands, Norway, and Turkey.

Leopard 2 Main Battle Tank

The Leopard 2 was developed from the MBT 70 program, a joint venture between the United States and the Federal Republic of Germany. The MBT 70 program, which was canceled in 1970, sought to identify future Soviet tank threats and develop a superior Main Battle Tank (MBT). Due to differing service requirements, the program to build a common MBT was abandoned in favor of an agreement to use common systems as much as possible. The Leopard 2 is considerably heavier, better armored, and better armed than the Leopard 1.

The hull is divided into three compartments: a driving compartment; a fighting compartment, which holds the commander, gunner, and loader; and an engine compartment. The massive turret houses a 120 millimeter smoothbore main gun built by Rheinmetall. The barrel is 17.4 feet long, making it 44 caliber. This same gun is also installed in the American M-1A1 Abrams under the interchangeable systems agreement; thus, American and West German ammunition is interchangeable. Both guns fire armor piercing, fin-stabilized, discarding sabot

tracer and tracer-phosphorus rounds (APFSDS-T, -T(P)), as well as high-explosive, antitank, multipurpose tracer and tracer-phosphorus rounds (HEAT-MP-T, -T(P)). The APFSDS ammunition is considered highly accurate at more than 2,000 yards. The 42 rounds of ammunition the Leopard 2 can carry are contained in semicombustible cases. The ammunition has a metal base to hold the primer. After firing, the empty shells are ejected into a container under the gun. The 120mm gun is semiautomatic, and the breech opens under recoil.

Left: This Leopard 2, belonging to the 43rd Armored Brigade of the Netherlands Army, participates in Operation Spearpoint tactical exercises near Einbach, West Germany, in August 1984. The Netherlands was the first foreign nation to purchase the Leopard 2. **Right:** The West German Leopard 2 mounts a 120mm smoothbore Rheinmetall main gun.

When the "war to end all wars" came to an end in 1918, the British people slowly woke to the fact that an entire generation of young Britons had been destroyed and their nation nearly bankrupted by four long years of war. Until the first air-raid warnings over England in September 1939, a deeply held spirit of pacifism possessed the nation, even as Hitler's strident voice and demonic visions drove the German people to rearm. Because the British did not, or would not, appreciate the threat rising in central Europe, they were ill-prepared to fight a new war.

When Germany invaded Poland on September 1, 1939, Britain had only a handful of modern ground and air weapons and not even enough rifles to equip an army that needed to be expanded rapidly. Fortunately, the so-called "Phony War" (a period during the winter of 1939–40 in which very little fighting occurred) on the western front provided nine months for British industries to catch up.

Still, when Hitler marched into Norway in April 1940 and Belgium, the Netherlands, and France the following month, the British Army could field only the 1st Army Tank Brigade, which consisted of the 4th and 7th Battalions of the Royal Tank Brigade. These two battalions had less than 160 tanks capable of meeting German tanks on equal terms. Seven other tank regiments already in France with the British Expeditionary Force were equipped with light tanks armed only with machine guns. The First Armored Division was still training in England. Only the 7th Battalion was equipped with a heavier tank; it had 23 Mark II Infantry Tanks out of a total of 50 tanks. (These Mark tanks should not be confused with Marks I through VIII of World War I.)

The Mark I Infantry Tank, nicknamed the Matilda, was designed in 1934. One specification for the Mark I was that it cost less than £6,000 ($25,500). This was only

met by using many such existing components as a Ford V-8 engine, which was barely suitable, and a suspension system designed for an earlier tank that weighed half as much. The Mark I was armed with a single .30 caliber machine gun, which was later up-gunned to .50 caliber.

The Spanish Civil War (1936–39) showed how ineffective a slow moving, lightly gunned, and lightly armored tank could be. In Germany, Russia, Japan, Italy, and, to a lesser extent, the United States, design work was pushed hard to develop a heavier, faster tank. The Mark II Infantry Tank, called the Matilda II, was Britain's improvement.

Trials on the new tank design had been completed by 1938 when rearmament began in earnest. Difficulties in obtaining the large castings for the turret and front armor plate, or glacis, delayed production. Thus, when the war began in September 1939, only two Mark IIs had been completed.

The Matilda II was a vast improvement over the original. The machine gun was replaced by a two-pounder (40 millimeter) gun. Armor thickness was increased to 3 inches and speed from eight to 15 miles per hour through the installation of two diesel engines. The one-man turret was retained because the tank's narrow body did not allow a wider turret.

The Mark II's first engagement with German armored forces occurred south of Arras, France. The 4th Royal Tank Brigade and the 7th Royal Tank Brigade, with the 7th Brigade's Mark IIs evenly distributed between the two brigades and both brigades supported by two reinforced infantry brigades, struck against Erwin Rommel's 7th Panzer Division and the SS Totenkopf Motorized Infantry Division. The Mark II's armor was proof against the 20mm guns of the Pz.Kpfw IIs

Left: A German bomb narrowly misses a British Matilda II tank in North Africa. **Right:** This Matilda II Infantry Tank Mark II wears the markings of the 7th Royal Tank Regiment. Shown here is the British camouflage paint scheme used in Egypt before WW II.

Cromwell A-27M Infantry Tank

By 1941 the British General Staff was convinced of the need for a tank that was faster and more heavily gunned than either the Matilda II or the Matilda II's replacement, the Churchill Infantry Tank, which could only travel at 15.5 miles per hour and was equipped with only a 40 millimeter gun. Experience in the Western Desert of North Africa showed that once enemy tanks were defeated, friendly tanks had to be able to fire high-explosive rounds in support of infantry. As a result, new specifications were published, and a fast tank useful in cavalry and infantry support roles was put into development.

After several false starts, the British General Staff settled on a tank design known as the Cromwell. It was to be powered by the Rolls Royce Merlin engine used in the Spitfire and Hurricane fighter aircraft but detuned from 1,075 to 600 horsepower. This was more than sufficient to move the Cromwell's 31 tons at speeds up to 40 miles per hour. This top speed was later reduced to 38 miles per hour when it was

discovered that the chassis could not withstand the faster speed.

A six-pounder (57mm) gun was selected as the main armament because it was considered powerful enough to penetrate German armor in frontal attacks. But the six pounder was found to be substandard when firing a high-explosive round against troops. The six pounder was also easily outranged by antitank gunners equipped with the 88mm antitank gun. A search was begun for a larger round and gun to provide the needed firepower.

By early 1943 the British had gained substantial experience with the American M-4 Sherman, which was equipped with a 75mm gun. The solution to the Cromwell's poor firepower was to use a gun similar to the Sherman's on the Cromwell. It helped that ammunition was plentiful from the American Lend Lease program and from captured Vichy French (the French government that collaborated with the Germans) stocks in Syria. The 57mm gun was bored out to accommodate the 75mm

round, the barrel was shortened, and a muzzle brake was added. Two BESA 7.92mm machine guns were also mounted, one in the turret coaxial with the main gun and the other in the hull. The limited scope of the hull machine gun made it of questionable value, and it was often left out in later production.

Early variations had carried different combinations of engines and main guns, but the new 75mm gunned tank driven by the Merlin Meteor engine was designated the Cromwell IV. The driver and hull gunner were contained in one compartment in the tank body; the commander, gunner, and loader occupied the turret. The interior was somewhat cramped, especially if the driver and hull gunner had to make a hasty exit. Later versions included an escape hatch for them.

From its introduction in early 1943 to the Normandy Invasion in June 1944, the Cromwell was used to train new tank crews. During Normandy, Cromwells

Left: The Mark VIII Cromwell Cruiser Tank was equipped with the new six-pounder gun and had a top speed of 32 mph. It went into production in 1943.
Right: An early Cromwell on gunnery trials in England.

141

went to France with the 7th Armored Division. Its combat debut was not a success. The Cromwell was initially stymied by the small operating area beyond the beachhead, which did not allow its best features—speed and agility—to be used until the breakout from Caen. After the Caen breakout, the Cromwell's Meteor engine became its greatest asset. It provided extreme agility and a good turn of speed and was very reliable. The Cromwell advanced at a rate of 70 miles per day after the breakout from the Normandy beachhead.

It had become obvious earlier than Normandy that the 75mm gun was no match for the heavy armor of the Pz.Kpfw V Panther and the Pz.Kpfw VI Tiger I, nor was the Cromwell's armor protection against their more powerful main guns. To deal with the latter, appliqué armor was bolted onto Cromwells to increase the tank's armor thickness from 2.5 inches to 3.9 inches.

The Cromwell's chief advantage remained its superior agility and speed when compared with German tanks or the American M-4 Sherman. While the Cromwell was not a match for the Panther in a toe-to-toe slugging match, it was fast and maneuverable enough to take a Panther out from behind.

The next step in up-rating the Cromwell was to mount a larger gun. But the chassis was considered too small to take a larger turret. The chassis was lengthened by a little more than five feet, and a new turret, mounting a 17-pounder (76.2mm high-velocity) gun, was added. This new tank was named the Challenger (not to be confused with the Main Battle Tank discussed later) and from its first appearance in early 1944 was used to support the Cromwell and provide heavy, long-range firepower.

But even the Challenger, with its more powerful gun, did not solve the problem of facing Panthers and Tiger Is. A new tank was designed and built based on the Cromwell plan. Called the Comet, it mounted the 77mm 49 caliber gun. The gun was capable of penetrating 4.3 inches of armor angled at 30° at 500 yards. The Comet reached the front lines in November 1944.

While the Cromwell was overshadowed by the American M-4 Sherman, which could outperform it in most respects, the Cromwell made an important contribution to British armored tactics and to the race across northern Europe.

Cromwell A-27M Infantry Tank	
Country:	Great Britain
Type:	Cruiser Tank, Medium
Dimensions	
Length:	6.4 m (21 ft)
Width:	3.05 m (10 ft)
Height:	2.48 m (8.16 ft)
Combat weight:	24,948 kg (27.5 tons)
Engine:	Rolls Royce Merlin Meteor V-12 gasoline
Armament:	One 75mm Mark V main gun; two 7.92mm BESA machine guns
Crew:	5
Speed:	61 km/h (38 mph)
Range:	278 km (173 mi)
Obstacle/grade performance:	0.9 m (3 ft)
Date of service:	1942

Left: Many Cromwell Cruiser Tanks, such as this one belonging to the Guards Armored Division (Welsh Guards), had their six-pounder (57mm) guns rebored to 75mm.
Right: The Cromwell was too lightly gunned to effectively deal with German Tigers and Panthers. A new version, mounting a seventeen-pounder (77mm) gun, appeared in November 1944. The Comet shown here belongs to the 1st Royal Tank Regiment.

Centurion Main Battle Tank

The Centurion's development began in 1943 when the British Army asked for a new cruiser tank equipped with at least a 17-pounder gun. They wanted a fast tank that, even though heavily armored, would perform well in cross-country travel. Prototypes of the new tank, known as the A-41, were built and sent to Germany in 1945, but the war ended before they saw combat.

At first, the Centurion, as the new tank was named, did not represent much, if any, improvement over medium tanks then available. In fact, it compared well with the German Panther, which had entered service two years earlier. The Centurion weighed 42.5 tons, the Panther Model D, 43. It was equipped with a 17-pounder 76.5 millimeter gun that had a muzzle velocity of 2,950 feet per second. The Panther D was armed with a 75mm gun with a muzzle velocity of 3,070 feet per second. The Centurion was powered by a 600

horsepower Rolls Royce Merlin Meteor V-12 engine, the Panther D used a 642 horsepower V-12 Maybach engine.

Even the next-generation Centurion seemed a shadow of the Panther. When the Centurion Mark (Mk) 3 (not to be confused with either the World War I Marks or the Matildas of World War II) was developed, it was equipped with an 83.4mm, or 20-pounder, gun. The up-rated Panther, which had design work completed but never entered production, was to be equipped with the 88mm gun used on the Tiger II. Both guns had muzzle velocities very close to 3,340 feet per second.

Even so, the Centurion 3 was the most heavily armed tank of its category in the immediate postwar years. But strangely enough, neither the tank's design nor even its gun design, was responsible for this. The Centurion 3 fired a new round that used a narrow diameter, finned, solid

steel spike or arrow that was wrapped in a light metal jacket to give it the same diameter as the bore. This new round was called an armor-piercing, discarding sabot (APDS) round, and it left the muzzle of the 20 pounder at 4,800 feet per second. It could penetrate twice as much armor as the 88mm gun.

The Centurion 3 was a commercial, as well as a military, success. It was adopted by Australia, Canada, India, South Africa, Sweden, Switzerland, and other nations. The Centurion was perhaps the first tank to face itself in a shooting war. Egypt, Iraq, and Israel bought Centurions and used them against one another in the 1967 and 1973 Arab–Israeli wars. The United States purchased Centurions and gave them to Denmark and the Netherlands under the Military Aid Program.

The Centurion 5, 6, 7, and 8 models were successively up-armored and up-

Left: The British Centurion entered service in 1945 and has since served in virtually every war zone from Burma to the Middle East. This Centurion, belonging to the Australian 1st Armored Regiment, moves up to Fire Support Base Coral, South Vietnam, in 1968. **Right:** An early Centurion Mark 2, armed with the seventeen-pounder gun and loaded with Australian troops, crosses the Imjin River during the Korean War.

gunned with the 105mm L7 series of guns. The final version, the Centurion 13, is equipped with the 105mm L7A2 gun, the same one used on the West German Leopard 1; the Israeli Merkava; the American M-48A5, M-60, and M-1 Abrams; the Japanese Type 74; and the Swedish Strv 103B Main Battle Tanks.

The Centurion's hull is divided into the usual three compartments. The driver's compartment is in front; the fighting compartment is in the center. The engine compartment is in the rear and separated from the other two compartments by a fireproof wall. The engine and transmission drive the rear sprockets. A Horstmann-type suspension system is used in which three units on a side each hold two road wheels on one set of concentric springs. Six return rollers are employed, but these are hard to see on the later model tanks since skirt armor for protection against high-explosive, antitank projectiles covers most of the tread.

The commander and gunner are seated on the right side of the turret, the loader on the left. The commander has a cupola that can be turned in a complete circle independently of the turret. The gunner's station has a periscope sight with aiming devices that are linked to the command-er's station. The loader's station has twin hatch covers and a periscope. Infrared searchlights and driving lights have been installed on later variations. Maximum armor thickness is 6 inches on the turret front and 4.6 inches on the hull glacis plate.

The L7A2 main gun has an effective range of 1,968 yards when using armor-piercing, discarding sabot rounds and 4,374 yards when using high-explosive squash head rounds. Trained crews can fire up to eight rounds per minute. The main gun is aimed using a coaxially mounted .50 caliber machine gun that fires tracers in three-round bursts up to a range of 1,968 yards. The gunner watches the tracer rounds through his periscope gun sight and sets the range on a drum device linked to the main gun. Two 7.62mm NATO machine guns are also carried, one mounted on the command-er's cupola and the other coaxially to the left side of the main gun for use against unarmored vehicles and enemy personnel. Later variations of the Centurion have 12 smoke dischargers, six mounted on either side of the turret.

The 13 models of the Centurion have been built by four manufacturers—Leyland Motors, the Royal Ordnance Factory at Leeds, the Royal Ordnance Factory at Woolwich, and Vickers, Ltd. Five other vehicles based on the Centurion have also been built. These include two Centurion Mk 5 Bridgelayers, the Centurion Mk 2 and Mk 5 Armored Recovery Vehicles, and the Centurion Beach Armored Recovery Vehicle.

Although the Centurion is now out of service with the British Army, it remains a potent punch in the arsenals of Denmark, Israel, Jordan, the Netherlands, South Africa, Somalia, Sweden, and Switzerland.

Centurion (Mk 13) Main Battle Tank	
Country:	Great Britain
Type:	Main Battle Tank
Dimensions	
Length:	7.82 m (25.7 ft)
Width:	3.39 m (11.1 ft)
Height:	3 m (9.87 ft)
Combat weight:	51,820 kg (57.1 tons)
Engine:	Rolls Royce Mk IVB V-12 gasoline
Armament:	One 105mm L7A2 main gun; two 7.62mm NATO machine guns; one .50 caliber ranging machine gun
Crew:	4
Speed:	34 km/h (21.5 mph)
Range:	190 km (118 mi)
Obstacle/grade performance:	0.9 m (3.0 ft)
Date of service:	1945

Left: These British Centurions wade ashore in the Middle East during an exercise. Thirteen nations have purchased the British Centurion. **Right:** The Mark 13 is the latest variation of the venerable British Centurion. It is equipped with a 105mm main gun, a ranging machine gun, and an infrared searchlight.

Chieftain Main Battle Tank

The Chieftain Main Battle Tank (MBT) derives from a long line of tanks that began with the Mark II Matilda II in 1939. Matilda's successors evolved from infantry support through cruiser to medium battle tank as they were made progressively faster and up-gunned—Matilda II (40 millimeter), Cromwell (57mm and 75mm), Comet (76mm), and Centurion (76.2mm, 83.4mm, and 105mm). Each succeeding design also grew heavier. The Centurion weighed in at nearly 57 tons and could move at only 22 miles per hour on the road.

In the late 1940s with the threat of the Soviet T-54/T-55 and the rumored T-62 in mind, designers at Leyland had intended the Chieftain MBT to replace both the Centurion Medium Tank and the Conqueror Heavy Tank. The resulting tank was an accommodation among firepower, speed, and agility.

The design of the Chieftain emphasized firepower and protection, but the price paid was less mobility. The Chieftain is a heavy tank at 60 tons and is considered underpowered, even with the larger 650 horsepower Leyland engine installed. The initial engine, a 585 horsepower diesel, was replaced in 1967.

The Chieftain's silhouette is two feet shorter than that of its forerunner, the Conqueror. Armor thicknesses are classified, but cast and rolled armor is used on the hull. The turret is cast in two pieces and then welded together. Appliqué armor provides additional turret protection at the front and behind the commander's cupola.

The hull is cast in three pieces, which are welded together, and, like earlier British tanks, divided into three compartments—driving, fighting, and engine,

front to back. The Chieftain carries a crew of four. The driver sits near the front in a reclining seat with a hatch to the right. The commander, gunner, and loader are in the turret, which contains a separate rotating cupola for the commander. The commander has full 360° vision through a variety of periscopes, which are also fitted with night vision devices.

Full nuclear-biological-chemical protection is provided through a forced-air filtering system. Two six-barreled smoke dischargers are mounted on the turret. An infrared searchlight is mounted to the right of the commander's cupola.

The new tank was built around the 120mm L11A5 rifled tank gun. When introduced in May 1963, the Chieftain was the most powerfully armed tank in the world. The British Army plans to re-equip its Chieftains with a new, even more pow-

Left: Some British Chieftain tanks have aluminum bulldozer blades mounted on the hull front for preparing defensive positions and clearing roads. **Right:** The Chieftain Main Battle Tank was armed with the 120mm L11A5 rifled main gun, which made it one of the most heavily armed MBTs of its time. The Chieftain is now being replaced in British service by the Challenger MBT.

erful L30 high-pressure rifled gun. The Chieftain is also equipped with three machine guns, a 12.7mm range-finding gun and two 7.62mm NATO machine guns, one coaxial and the other, which is mounted within reach of the commander's cupola, for antiaircraft use. The range finding machine gun was used to aim the main gun before the Barr and Stroud laser sight was installed. Most of the range finding guns have been removed. All Chieftains have a fully integrated fire control system, which allows the 120mm main gun to be fired accurately either out to 2,000 meters while moving or out to 3,000 meters while stationary.

The Chieftain has been used widely throughout the world by Great Britain as well as other nations. One of the better customers for the Chieftain was Iran prior to 1978. Starting in 1971, Iran bought nearly 900 Chieftains, and all were delivered before the Shah's government fell in 1979. The Chieftain saw a great deal of service in the Iran–Iraq War of 1980–88 and gave a very good account of itself against Soviet tanks. Iraq is said to have captured more than 300 Chieftains during the fighting, a large number of which were undamaged because they were abandoned by their crews. Chieftains have also been purchased by Jordan, Oman, Iraq, and Kuwait. The refusal of Great Britain to sell Chieftain tanks to Israel during and after the 1967 Arab–Israeli war prompted Israel to develop its own MBT, the Merkava.

Chieftain Main Battle Tank	
Country:	Great Britain
Type:	Main Battle Tank
Dimensions	
Length:	7.52 m (24.7 ft)
Width:	3.33 m (10.1 ft)
Height:	2.90 m (9.5 ft)
Combat weight:	55,000 kg (60.6 tons)
Engine:	Leyland L60 No. 4, Mk 8A
Armament:	One 120mm 55 caliber L115A rifled gun; two 7.62mm NATO machine guns, coaxial and antiaircraft; one 12.7mm ranging machine gun
Crew:	4
Speed:	48 km/h (30 mph)
Range:	500 km (300 mi)
Obstacle/grade performance:	0.9 m (3 ft)
Date of service:	1963

Left: A Chieftain MBT belonging to the 17/21st Lancers, British Army of the Rhine. **Right:** More than 1,900 Chieftains were built in the United Kingdom, 900 for British forces and the remainder for several other countries. The Chieftain is currently in service with the United Kingdom, Iran, Iraq, Kuwait, Oman, and Jordan.

Challenger Main Battle Tank

In the late 1960s an assessment of present and future Soviet armor capability galvanized the major NATO nations into a series of new tank development programs. The United States and West Germany, and Great Britain and West Germany collaborated on new Main Battle Tank (MBT) designs to meet the Soviet threat into the first decade of the next century. But different technological approaches, army needs, and budget considerations brought an end to the partnerships. Nevertheless, three new MBTs did result from the various joint development programs: the West German Leopard 2, the American M-1 Abrams, and the British Challenger.

Development of the Challenger, considered a successor to the Chieftain, can be said to have begun as early as 1968. The requirements for a new MBT were defined in full by 1978, and by 1980 the main gun and the engine had been selected. The Challenger became operational in 1983 and is now being built by the Royal Ordnance Factory at Leeds, England.

Like its predecessor, the Chieftain, the Challenger is an accommodation of firepower, armor protection, and speed and agility. The internal layout is similar to the Chieftain's. A Rolls Royce 12 cylinder diesel engine that puts out 1,200 horsepower

at 2,300 rpm turns the rear-mounted drive sprockets. The Challenger is a bit faster than the Chieftain despite being eight tons heavier.

The turret and hull are heavily armored; the exact thickness figures are classified. Chobham armor is used, as well as steel plate armor in the hull and turret. Chobham armor is a classified mix of plastic, ceramic, and steel plates designed to absorb and deflect kinetic rounds and prevent the effective use of shaped-charge gas plasma jets.

The Challenger has a classified state-of-the-art gunnery and sighting system that

Left: The Challenger Main Battle Tank is the latest MBT in British Service and among the most powerful in the world. **Right:** The hull and turret of the Challenger MBT incorporate Chobham armor, a steel and ceramic mix.

incorporates a laser range finder and a thermal imaging system for use at night, in smoke, or in fog. A new gun sighting system known as TOGS—Thermal Observation and Gunnery System—is now being installed in all Challenger tanks.

The Challenger's main armament is the 120 millimeter L11A5 rifled gun, the same that had been thoroughly tested and proved in the Chieftain. The tank carries up to 58 rounds of four different two-piece types. The four types normally carried in various mixes are: armor-piercing, discarding sabot-tracer (APDS-T) with a muzzle velocity of 4,495 feet per second; discarding sabot-tracer (DS-T) with a velocity similar to the APDS-T; high-explosive squash head-tracer (HESH-T) with a muzzle velocity of 2,198 feet per second;

and smoke-white phosphorus (SMOKE-WP) with a velocity similar to the HESH-T round. In addition to the main gun, the Challenger is equipped with two 7.62mm NATO machine guns, one mounted coaxially with the main gun, the other near the commander's cupola.

The Challenger's fire control system, based on those developed for the Chieftain, does not seem to be as accurate or as fast as that of the Leopard 2 or the M-1 Abrams. The British Challenger team has finished last in each Canada Army Trophy NATO gunnery competition between 1983 and 1987. The TOGS sight cannot scan independently of the turret's own movement, reducing the commander's ability to search for new targets while the gunner fires on the current target.

The Challenger's lack of mobility is another factor against it. The Leopard 2 and the M-1 Abrams are capable of speeds in excess of 40 miles per hour, which is at least five miles per hour faster than the Challenger's top speed. The Soviet T-64/T-72/T-80 series is from three to six miles per hour faster than the Challenger.

The Challenger is too new an MBT for firm judgments at this point. It follows the practice of past, and very successful, British tanks being far more heavily armored and gunned than its potential enemies.

Challenger Main Battle Tank	
Country:	Great Britain
Type:	Main Battle Tank
Dimensions	
Length:	8.33 m (27.4 ft)
Width:	3.42 m (11.25 ft)
Height:	2.5 m (8.16 ft)
Combat weight:	62,000 kg (68.3 tons)
Engine:	Rolls Royce Condor V-12 diesel
Armament:	One 120mm 55 caliber L115A rifled gun; two 7.62mm NATO machine guns, coaxial and antiaircraft
Crew:	4
Speed:	56 km/h (35 mph)
Range:	350 km (250 mi)
Obstacle/grade performance:	0.9 m (3 ft)
Date of service:	1983

Left: Like all Challengers, this one, shown maneuvering at the Royal Armored Corps Test Center, Bovington Camp, Dorset, is armed with the L11A5 120mm rifled main gun. **Right:** The Challenger has a fully integrated and computerized fire control system that employs a laser range finder able to accurately measure distances up to 11,000 yards.

AMX-13 Light Tank

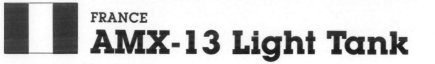

In 1946, when design work on the AMX-13 began, the tank was intended to be a destroyer/reconnaissance vehicle. As the tank neared development, the manufacturer, Atelier de Construction Roanne (ARE), modified the design slightly and produced a true light tank.

The hull of the AMX-13 is all welded and is divided into three compartments: The driver and engine compartments are located at the front, and the turret is mounted at the rear. Probably the most distinguishing feature of the AMX-13 is its Fives-Cail Babcock two-part oscillating turret. The main gun is fixed in position in the upper half of the turret; to elevate or depress the gun, the upper half is pivoted onto the lower half. Use of this oscillating turret permits the adoption of an automatic revolver loading system in which each magazine holds six rounds.

Initially, the main gun for the tank was the standard 75 millimeter cannon with a single baffle muzzle brake. The gun had a rate of fire of one round every five seconds until the two six-round magazines were empty. Once the rounds were discharged, the magazines had to be re-

filled by hand outside the tank. The tank carried a total of 37 rounds of ammunition and also sported either a 7.5mm or 7.62mm machine gun that was mounted coaxially on the right side of the main gun. Another machine gun can be mounted externally near the commander's position. The tank also has a total of four electrically operated smoke dischargers, two on either side of the turret.

None of the AMX-13 tanks are equipped to operate in a nuclear-biological-chemical warfare environment, and only a few countries have outfitted the tank with any sort of night fighting/detection equipment or sensors. Many of the nearly 20 different countries using the tank have retrofitted their inventory of tanks with either the larger 90mm or 105mm guns.

AMX-13 tanks armed with the 90mm gun first entered service in the mid-1960s, and all tanks in the French Army were retrofitted with this cannon by the early 1970s. With the larger gun, the tank carries 34 rounds of ammunition of which 21 are carried in the turret—12 in the magazine. The combination of the 105mm rifled gun and the FL-12 armored turret was developed exclusively for the export marketplace.

Depending upon a nation's individual needs, the AMX-13 comes with either a diesel or gasoline power plant and a five-speed manual transmission. In terms of more modern light tanks, the AMX-13 has a competitive range of around 350 to 400 kilometers with its gasoline engine and 550 to 600 kilometers with the diesel power plant.

Although its technology may be dated, the AMX-13 has remained a viable choice for many smaller nations seeking a proven tank design that can also be adapted for use as an armored personnel carrier, an air-defense vehicle, an armored recovery vehicle, and even a self-propelled howitzer.

AMX-13 Light Tank	
Country:	France
Type:	Light Tank
Dimensions	
Length:	4.88 m (16 ft)
Width:	2.5 m (8.2 ft)
Height:	2.3 m (7.5 ft)
Combat weight:	15,000 kg (16.5 tons)
Engine:	SOFAM Model 8G × b 8 cylinder horizontally opposed gasoline or Detroit Diesel 6V-53T water-cooled turbocharged V-6 diesel or Baudouin 6F 11 SRY water-cooled turbocharged V-6 diesel
Armament:	One 75mm main gun, or one 90mm main gun, or one 105mm main gun; two 7.5mm or 7.62mm NATO machine guns
Crew:	3
Speed:	**Gas:** 60 km/h (37 mph) **Diesel:** 64 km/h (39 mph)
Range:	**Gas:** 350–400 km (217–248 mi) **Diesel:** 550–600 km (341–372 mi)
Obstacle/grade performance:	0.65 m (2.1 ft)
Date of service:	1952

Left: The French AMX-13 is a light tank used as a tank destroyer and for reconnaissance. It has an oscillating turret, and its 90mm main gun is equipped with an automatic loader. **Right:** The French AMX-13 has been widely sold to other nations. At least 25 armies now use the AMX-13, including El Salvador and Switzerland.

AMX-30 Main Battle Tank

The AMX-30 is the principal Main Battle Tank (MBT) for the French Army. Development began in the mid-1950s as a joint Franco–German MBT. The first of two prototypes was completed in 1960, but the joint cooperation between the two nations did not materialize. Adopted by the French Army in 1963, the tank went into production in 1966 and was built to replace the aging American-supplied M-47 tanks.

The tank's hull is made of rolled steel plates that are welded together and divided into three compartments. The driver is seated in front on the left side, while the remaining three crewmembers—gunner, loader, and commander—are seated in the turret. Unique to the tank is its Renault-produced Hispano-Suiza 12 cylinder, water-cooled supercharged engine that can operate on oil, petrol, or paraffin. In addition, this multifueled power plant, its gearbox, clutch, and steering unit can be removed for replacement in less than 45 minutes.

The main gun on the AMX-30 is the 105 millimeter CN-105-F1. The gun has neither a muzzle brake nor a fume extractor but is fitted with a magnesium alloy thermal heat sleeve. The tank uses a compressed air system to blow any fumes from the barrel. The gun's recoil equipment is made up of two diametrically opposed hydraulic brakes and a counter recoil barrel system. The AMX-30 carries a total of 47 rounds of ammunition, 19 of which are stored in the turret area, while an additional 28 are located to the right of the driver in the tank's hull.

In addition to its powerful main gun, the AMX-30 has its own built-in anti-air defense system in the form of a 20mm Model F2 cannon located on the left side of the main armament. Capable of being elevated 40° higher than the main gun, the M693 cannon has an effective range of nearly 1,500 meters and can fire hundreds of high-explosive incendiary or armor-piercing rounds at low-flying attack helicopters or fixed-wing aircraft. Additional armament includes a commander's 7.62mm Model F1 machine gun and a total of four smoke dischargers, with two mounted on either side of the turret. The smoke dischargers can lay an effective smoke screen in less than three seconds and totally hide the tank in less than eight seconds.

Outfitted with a self-contained nuclear-biological-chemical protection system, the AMX-30 is currently undergoing an upgrade to the AMX-30 B2 configuration. In addition to a new gearbox that increases the tank's on-the-spot turning ability and allows shifting when turning around bends, the upgrade package also includes new laser range finder options, boosted power plant outputs, and a beefed-up suspension system.

All 1,084 AMX-30 tanks in the French inventory will be upgraded to the B2 configuration by 1993. With the new laser range finder fire control system, once a day the tank commander will insert information about the type of ammunition to be used, drift angles, temperature, altitude, cross-wind velocity, and humidity. With the information stored in the tank's computers, the fire control system will calculate the target's distance, speed, and even the lead necessary to engage and destroy it.

With the upgrade modifications, the AMX-30 B2 will remain the French Army's MBT until replaced by the Leclerc MBT currently under development. For the nations that currently use the remaining 900 AMX-30 tanks, France is beginning to offer the basic B2 retrofits, along with a host of additional options—improved nuclear-biological-chemical protection capabilities, new day/night gyrostabilized sights, thicker gun shields, and additional appliqué armor protection plates.

AMX-30 Main Battle Tank	
Country:	France
Type:	Main Battle Tank
Dimensions	
Length:	6.59 m (21.6 ft)
Width:	3.1 m (10.1 ft)
Height:	2.29 m (7.5 ft)
Combat weight:	**AMX-30:** 36,000 kg (39.7 tons) **B2:** 37,000 kg (40.8 tons)
Engine:	Renault Hispano-Suiza 110 water-cooled 12 cylinder multifuel
Armament:	One 105mm rifled main gun; one 20mm Model 2 Type M693 air-defense cannon; one 7.62mm NATO machine gun
Crew:	4
Speed:	65 km/h (40 mph)
Range:	**AMX-30:** 500–600 km (310–372 mi) **B2:** 400–500 km (248–310 mi)
Obstacle/grade performance:	0.93 m (3 ft)
Date of service:	1966

Right: The AMX-30 is France's most widely deployed Main Battle Tank. It resulted from design work begun in the 1950s under a joint Franco–German agreement.

Leclerc Main Battle Tank

Following the collapse of yet another Franco–German Main Battle Tank (MBT) project in 1982, the French Prime Minister called for a successor to the current AMX-30 and AMX-30 B2 MBTs that are in use by the French Army. In answer to that call for a new-generation tank, the Atelier de Construction Roanne (ARE) is developing the Leclerc, which will begin production in 1990.

The Leclerc will be the first of the new generation of tanks in which the profile and silhouette will be lower and shorter to reduce and minimize vulnerability to hostile fire. The tank will still sport a conventional layout: The driver will continue to sit at the front; the low-profile turret remains in the center; and the power train is located at the rear. Use of an autoloader system designed by Creusot-Loire Industrie reduces the crew size to three—gunner, driver, and commander.

Main armament for the tank will be the 120 millimeter GIAT smoothbore gun. Up to 22 rounds of high-explosive, antitank or armor-piercing, fin-stabilized, discarding sabot ammunition with semicombustible cartridge case (the cartridge case burns up while still in the barrel after firing) can be carried in the turret bustle. Ammunition in the turret is separated from the crew by bulkheads and blow-out panels that are fitted into the roof. An additional 18 rounds will be carried in the tank hull. While the 120mm GIAT gun is slightly longer than the 120mm Rheinmetall gun in use on the German Leopard 2 and the American M-1A1 Abrams tank, it actually has a shorter recoil, as well as a new breech mechanism. Ammunition used by the Leopard 2 and M-1A1 tank is interchangeable with the Leclerc.

In addition to a smaller and lightweight design, the Leclerc also has a new high-technology fire control system that many estimate will account for an unprecedented 50 percent of the tank's total cost. The system will include a modular thermal image camera, laser range finder, and stabilized sights for the commander and gunner. All of this provides the crew with the ability to engage up to five different targets—both stationary and moving—within 60 seconds, while the Leclerc itself is traveling either on the road or cross-country. If the fire control system works the way it is being touted, the gunner should expect an unbelievable 95 to 98 percent probability of a first-round hit.

Standard equipment on the Leclerc will include a newly designed nuclear-biological-chemical protection system, a built-in snorkel for crossing deep water, fire detection and suppression systems for both the crew and engine compartments, a new secure communications system, and a new high-performance diesel engine to increase the Leclerc's overall operating capabilities.

While no firm details about the tank's armor have been released, it was originally believed to have a thin steel hull upon which a layer of explosive reactive armor would be added. In addition, multiple layers of reactive armor atop the turret would be installed to defeat the new generation of weapons that attack the top of a tank. Recently, however, new information has surfaced that leads international armor experts to believe that the Leclerc is likely to have a combination of laminate armor mixed with explosive reactive armor. Utilizing either of these two approaches will enable the Leclerc to be up-armored to meet future threats without substantially lowering its already high power-to-weight ratio.

It is expected the French will need between 1,100 and 1,500 Leclerc tanks. Once the vehicle enters production, it should peak at approximately ten new tanks a month. The first group to receive the new Leclerc has already been announced; it will be the French 2nd Armored Division, which will obtain it in 1992. Like all postwar French armored vehicles and tanks, the Leclerc will be available in an export version.

Leclerc Main Battle Tank	
Country:	France
Type:	Main Battle Tank
Dimensions	
Length:	6.6 m (21.6 ft)
Width:	3.3 m (10.8 ft)
Height:	2.3 m (7.5 ft)
Combat weight:	50,000–53,000 kg (55.1–58.4 tons)
Engine:	Uni Diesel V8X-1500 Hyperbar diesel
Armament:	One 120mm GIAT smoothbore main gun; one 12.7mm machine gun; one 7.62mm machine gun
Crew:	3
Speed:	70–75 km/h (43–46 mph) (projected)
Range:	550 km (341 mi) (projected)
Obstacle/grade performance:	Undisclosed
Date of service:	1992 (projected)

Over the last ten years, Engesa Engenheiros Especialdros S.A. São Paulo has established itself as one of the world's principal manufacturers of wheeled armored vehicles. Engesa's most recent achievement is the design and manufacture of a fully functional Main Battle Tank that was developed within an extremely short period of time. This new tank has successfully completed a host of competitive tests against some of the best-known tanks throughout the free world.

Known as the EE-T1 Osorio, the tank was developed to meet the requirements of the home and export marketplaces. Two prototype models have been built thus far. The first version was delivered to the Brazilian Army in the spring of 1985. This P.1 version is fitted with the Royal Ordnance 105 millimeter L7A3 gun and a modified recoil system. The second version, called the P.2, is armed with the more powerful 120mm smoothbore GIAT gun system, representing a more expensive export version with a more sophisticated fire control system.

After development studies that began in late 1982, the EE-T1 P.2, with its powerful 120mm smoothbore cannon, went into direct competition in front of the Saudi Arabian armed forces in 1985. It competed against such notable tanks as the British Challenger, the French AMX-30, and even the American M-1A1.

According to the Engesa directors, the EE-T1 Osorio is a state-of-the-art basic design that can be adapted to an individual country's requirements. With an eye toward the open and lucrative export marketplace, the Osorio was designed to be capable of modernization to meet future threats and install newly available technology.

To survive on the modern battlefield, the Osorio P.1 and P.2 tanks sport a combination of bi-metallic plate and composite plate armor. Both types of armor have been designed and built exclusively by Engesa engineers. The P.1, with its 105mm rifled gun, carries up to 12 rounds in the turret within easy reach of the loader. An additional 33 rounds are stored below in the front of the hull. The ammunition compartment in the turret is separated from the crew by a sliding door. The compartment has blow-off panels in the top area to prevent explosive hits that could ignite the stored rounds. The 105mm gun is fitted with the usual fume extractor, the Vicker-designed lightweight thermal heat sleeve, and muzzle reference mirror system. The more heavily armed P.2 Osorio, with its 120mm GIAT smoothbore, makes it comparable with any tank in production throughout the free world. Up-gunned to meet the threats of today and tomorrow, the Osorio P.2 also carries 12 rounds in the turret storage area and up to 26 additional rounds in the ammunition bin located in the front of the hull.

Two fire-control options are offered. The standard is a day/night gunner's periscope with a laser range finder and a day/night commander's periscope. At any time, the commander can override the gunner's controls, take aim, and fire. The more advanced fire control system has a gyrostabilized periscope with a laser range finder that allows the main gun to be fired while the tank is moving.

Both versions come with a V-12 turbocharged, water-cooled diesel power plant and fully automatic transmission. Each side of the tank sports six dual rubber-tire road wheels. While not ready for the racetrack, the tank accelerates from 0 to 30 miles per hour in about 17 seconds.

All development studies of the EE-T1 have been completed, and Engesa is now ready to begin production. The company is already looking at the possibility of installing a larger 155mm cannon, as well as offering an antiaircraft model.

EE-T1 Osorio Main Battle Tank	
Country:	Brazil
Type:	Main Battle Tank
Dimensions	
Length:	7.13 m (23.4 ft)
Width:	3.26 m (10.7 ft)
Height:	2.37 m (7.8 ft)
Combat weight:	**P.1:** 44,440 kg (48.9 tons) **P.2:** 44,700 kg (49.25 tons)
Engine:	MWM TBD 234 V-12 turbocharged water-cooled diesel
Armament:	**P.1:** one 105mm L7A3 rifled **P.2:** one 120mm GIAT smoothbore **P.1 and P.2:** one 7.62mm NATO machine gun
Crew:	4
Speed:	70 km/h (43 mph)
Range:	550 km (341 mi)
Obstacle/grade performance:	1.15 m (3.8 ft)
Date of service:	Ready for production

The state of Israel came into being in 1948, and almost immediately an alliance of Arab nations declared war. Since then, Israel has existed in a technical state of war with each of its Arab neighbors except Egypt. Israel has fought five major wars in defense of its right to exist—1948, 1956, 1967, 1973, and 1982, when Israel invaded southern Lebanon to drive out Palestinian terrorists.

Israel and the surrounding area are either desert or rolling hills, which form ideal tank country. During and after the 1967 War, Britain and France refused to supply certain categories of modern weapons to Israel. Alarmed, the Israeli government established a native defense industry so that state security would not be compromised by the political whims of outsiders. High priority was given to the development of a Main Battle Tank (MBT). The Merkava, which means "chariot" in Hebrew, was the result.

The Merkava combines the best features of American, British, French, and (captured) Soviet tanks, all of which have been used extensively by Israel in the past. The 1967 War reemphasized that armor protection is extremely important for tanks; so much so that Israeli designers placed tank survivability first, armament next, and speed third. General Israel Tal assumed command of the tank development project in 1970 and brought a professional soldier's experience to the design process. Merkava production began in 1978, and the new tank reached service units the following year.

For a tank that does not have an autoloading main gun and carries a crew of four, the Merkava has an extremely low silhouette. Its Horstmann-style suspension system makes it one of the most mobile off-road tanks in the world today. The Merkava I and Merkava II are equipped with a 105 millimeter gun, which is small by today's MBT standards. But the Merkavas fire Hetz armor-piercing, fin-stabi-

lized, discarding sabot rounds, which can penetrate MBT armor at ranges greater than 5,000 yards. The tank is equipped with a laser range finder that is connected to a ballistic computer that gives the tank first-round hit capability.

Israeli innovations in three other areas contribute to the Merkava's effectiveness: reactive and heavy armor, enhanced crew protection, and efficient and simple maintenance and repair procedures. Armor descriptions and thicknesses are classified, but Israeli statistics compiled after the 1982 invasion of Lebanon show that there is a 61 percent chance that a round striking a tank will penetrate; during the invasion of Lebanon only 41 percent of rounds striking the Merkava penetrated. Of rounds striking a tank, there is a 30 percent chance of penetration into the crew compartment; only 13 percent of all rounds striking a Merkava penetrated the crew compartments. This was due to the placement of the Merkava's engine up front and the thickness of the glacis armor belt. Normally, 31 percent of all hits set a tank on fire, and fire destroys the tank 85 to 90 percent of the time. Only 15 percent of all hits caused fires in Merkavas, and only one Merkava was lost to fire as far as is known.

The Merkava was designed with fully armored, self-sealing fuel tanks; fireproof containers that provide one hour minimum protection for all ammunition; and a heavily armored crew compartment. All crewmembers are required to wear protective asbestos clothing, and the tanks are equipped with an extremely fast-reacting fire suppression system built by Spectronix.

Israeli Defense Force armor records show that no Merkava was out of action for more than 48 hours, while M-60, Centurion, or T-62 tanks could require up to two weeks to repair. The battle-tested Merkava is truly a superior MBT.

Merkava	
Country:	Israel
Type:	Main Battle Tank
Dimensions	
Length:	7.5 m (24.4 ft)
Width:	3.7 m (12.2 ft)
Height:	2.75 m (9 ft)
Combat weight:	**Merkava I:** 60,000 kg (66.1 tons) **Merkava II and Merkava III:** Classified
Engine	**Merkava I:** Teledyne Continental V-12 diesel 900 hp **Merkava II:** Teledyne Continental V-12 diesel 1,200 hp **Merkava III:** Unknown, believed to be 1,400 to 1,500 hp
Armament:	**Merkava I:** One 105mm M68 rifled **Merkava II:** One 105mm M68 rifled **Merkava III:** One 120mm smoothbore **Merkava I, II, and III:** Three 7.62mm NATO machine guns; one 60mm mortar
Crew:	4
Speed:	46 km/h (28.6 mph)
Range:	400 km (249 mi)
Obstacle/grade performance:	0.95 m (3.1 ft)
Date of service	**Merkava I:** 1979 **Merkava II:** 1983 **Merkava III:** 1987

Right: The Israeli Merkava was designed with a low hull and turret silhouette, engine in front for additional armor protection, and a 105mm main gun. Shown here is the uprated Merkava II. **Bottom left:** The Israeli Merkava I Main Battle Tank proved far superior to the Soviet T-62 in Syrian hands during the 1982 invasion of Lebanon. This Merkava I moves along the Northern Road in southern Lebanon on routine patrol.

Stridsvagn 103 Main Battle Tank

Stridsvagn—battle car in Swedish—103 series tank is a highly capable Main Battle Tank (MBT) in a 43-ton package. The Strv 103, or S tank as it is also known, is the first practical turretless MBT to be developed. The low profile makes the Strv 103 very difficult to see when on the move and almost impossible to find when lying hull-down in ambush.

Design work began on the S tank in the mid-1950s. Sweden sought a tank suited to its particular landscape—a small country with rolling farmland in the south and high forests and tundra, which is frozen in the winter and soggy in the summer, in the north. A tank was needed that could operate across this kind of surface without bogging down. The tank also had to be able to meet the threat of both Warsaw Pact and NATO tanks.

The Swedish S tank design differs from earlier German and Soviet turretless armored vehicles in that its main gun is fixed in its mounting. This eliminates the need for the heavy mantlet and surrounding armor. It also makes possible the installation of a lightweight, reliable automatic loader and the elimination of one crew position. The S tank carries heavy frontal armor, the composition and thicknesses of which remain classified. During a 1984 upgrade program, add-on armor was applied to the Strv 103, particularly in this area.

Since the S tank must stop to fire, the driver can serve as loader and gunner. The driver/gunner sits on the left side, the commander on the right. Both have a complete set of driving and gunnery controls, and the commander can override the driver/gunner's controls at any time. Seated backward and slightly behind the driver is the radio operator, who also has a set of controls for driving the tank backward.

A unique characteristic of the S Tank is its two engines. The main engine was originally a six cylinder Detroit Diesel engine. The secondary engine, used for boost power in combat or for cold-weather starting, was a gas turbine Boeing Model 553 that delivered 490 horsepower. The combined output of both engines compares favorably with MBTs with heavier engines that consume more fuel. As part of the total upgrade of all Strv Bs to Strv Cs that began in 1984, a new Rolls Royce K60 diesel replaced the Detroit Diesel engine. The engines are located up front to provide additional protection to the crew of three, who are contained entirely within the hull.

The Swedish-designed 62 caliber 105 millimeter main gun is fed from a magazine holding 50 rounds. With the automatic loader, up to 15 rounds can be fired per minute. The automatic loader ejects spent cases outside the tank. If the automatic loader fails, it can be hand cranked by the radio operator. Two crewmembers can reload the magazine through the rear hatches in ten minutes.

The main gun is aimed by lowering or raising the hull on a special hydraulic suspension system developed in Sweden. Traversing the gun is done by turning the tank. Until the advent of the laser range finder and advanced ballistic computers and fire control systems, this was not a drawback since all tanks had to stop to fire accurately. Today, state-of-the-art MBTs like the Merkava II, the M-1A1 Abrams, the British Challenger, and the Soviet T-64/T-72/T-80 series can fire while on the move, but the tracks of the S tank lock when the main gun is fired.

Two 7.62mm fixed machine guns are mounted on the left side of the hull. A third machine gun is mounted outside the commander's cupola but can be fired automatically from within the hull.

Each Strv 103C tank carries a bulldozer blade folded back under the nose that can be deployed and operated from inside the tank. Each tank is also fitted with a flotation screen that can be rigged in 20 minutes. This allows the tank to ford streams and rivers at nearly four miles per hour, using its tracks for propulsion.

Some aspects of Strv 103C MBT have been copied by other countries, but to date Sweden is the only nation employing a true turretless MBT. The United States and the Soviet Union are known to be developing turretless models for the next generation of MBTs.

Stridsvagen 103C Main Battle Tank	
Country:	Sweden
Type:	Main Battle Tank
Dimensions	
Length:	7.04 m (23.1 ft)
Width:	3.6 m (11.8 ft)
Height:	2.14 m (7 ft)
Combat weight:	39,700 kg (43.8 tons)
Engine:	One Rolls Royce K60 diesel; one Boeing M553 gas turbine
Armament:	One 105mm L71 Bofors main gun; three 7.62mm Ksp 58 machine guns
Crew:	3
Speed:	50 km/h (31 mph)
Range:	390 km (242 mi)
Obstacle/grade performance:	0.9 m (3 ft)
Date of service:	1966

Right: The Swedish turretless Stridsvagn 103 Main Battle Tank carries a bulldozer blade under its nose for preparing defensive positions and for clearing mines and obstacles. **Bottom left:** This S-103 has its flotation screen raised. The driver steers the tank by standing on the highest point of the tank, peering over the screen, and using a remote throttle and reins attached to the tiller bar.

Infanterikanonvagn 91

Sweden, a neutral country at the top of Europe, is the key to northern Europe. It is in the rather unique position of having to defend itself from two sides in the event of a European war—from incursions by the Warsaw Pact and/or the North Atlantic Treaty Organization (NATO). To maintain its traditional neutrality, the Swedish government is determined to defend its borders against *anyone* attempting to transgress.

The nature of Sweden's terrain—wooded uplands and tundra in the north, rolling farmland in the center and south—is ideal tank country. During World War II, the Swedish Army paid close attention to developments in armored warfare and in the postwar years purchased 80 British Centurions, which were designated as Strv 81.

Tank development in Sweden has been affected by two considerations. First, Sweden cannot compete with the two major power blocs in development and production costs. Second, funds spent for defense should be spent inside Sweden as much as possible. Therefore, low-cost solutions to armored warfare have been sought.

Sweden has followed two directions as its tank development has evolved. In one direction, Sweden has pursued the Main Battle Tank (MBT) but redesigned the MBT to fit its needs. The other direction has led to the tank destroyer, which was pioneered by Germany during World War II. One class of tank destroyers is a lightweight, lightly armored vehicle similar to the World War II vehicles Pz.Kpfw 38(t), the Marder III *Panzerjager*, and the *Jagdpanzer* 38(t) Hetzer. Each of these mounted powerful high-velocity guns with the express purpose of protecting infantry by destroying enemy tanks. Tank destroyers evaded destruction themselves by speed, agility, and outgunning and outranging their opponent. Since light weight and light armor do not re-

quire a heavy chassis/hull combination, a lighter, cheaper, and easier-to-maintain engine can be used. All of this drastically reduces the cost of the tank.

Infanterikanonvagn 91 (Ikv-91) is the fourth and most technologically advanced in a series of fast, agile, lightly armored, and powerfully gunned tanks that the Swedes have built since the end of World War II. The Ikv-91 is an 18-ton tank driven by a Volvo six cylinder, turbocharged diesel engine that provides a road speed of 40 miles per hour and a cross-country speed that remains classified. The Ikv-91's low ground pressure (less than seven pounds per square inch) permits it to operate over summer tundra and winter snow at a faster speed than far heavier MBTs could.

It carries a 90 millimeter main gun manufactured by Bofors that fires either high-explosive or high-explosive, fin-stabilized antitank rounds at nearly 4,500 feet per second. A total of 59 rounds can be stored in the hull and turret. The main gun is connected to a computerized fire control system and a laser range finder. Armor type and thicknesses are classified, but the vehicle is lightly armored to keep its weight down. Two Browning 7.62mm NATO machine guns manufactured in Sweden are carried, one mounted coaxially with the main gun, the other mounted on the turret. A total of 12 grenade launchers, six on either side of the wedge-shaped turret, can fire either smoke or standard antipersonnel grenades. Sweden fields 20 companies of Ikv-91 tank destroyers in two brigades.

Production began in 1975 and was completed by 1978. An export version, which has improved armor protection and carries a 105mm gun, has been built by the Swedish company Hägglund and Soner.

Infanterikanonvagn 91	
Country:	Sweden
Type:	Tank Destroyer
Dimensions	
Length:	6.41 m (21 ft)
Width:	3 m (9.8 ft)
Height:	2.32 m (7.6 ft)
Combat weight:	16,300 kg (18 tons)
Engine:	Volvo-Penta TD 120 six cylinder turbocharged diesel
Armament:	One 90mm Bofors main gun; two 7.62mm NATO Browning machine guns
Crew:	4
Speed:	65 km/h (40 mph)
Range:	500 km (310 mi)
Obstacle/grade performance:	0.8 m (2.6 ft)
Date of service:	1975

Right: The Ikv-91 tank destroyer is completely amphibious. Its caterpillar tracks propel it at about three mph. This amphibious capability is a plus in Sweden, where lakes and streams are so prevalent.

OF-40 Main Battle Tank

The Italian OF-40 Main Battle Tank (MBT) was produced as a private joint venture between OTO Melara and Fiat. The first prototype OF-40 (O for OTO Melara, F for Fiat, and 40 for the approximate weight of the tank) was built in 1980. It was an attempt by the two companies to join technologies in breaking into the tank export marketplace by producing a relatively simple vehicle that was made from a mixture of "off-the-shelf" indigenous- and foreign-design components. The idea was to produce an MBT that would supply adequate firepower and mobility without draining the coffers of a buying nation.

In terms of general appearance, the OF-40 resembles the German Leopard 1A4 and actually uses components from the Leopard tank. The interior of the all-welded hull is divided into three compartments: The driver sits at the front; the turret is located in the center; and the engine/drivetrain is at the rear. In the turret, the loader is located on the left, and the commander and gunner are located on the right. Up top, the commander does not have a traditional cupola, but a day/night sight, stabilized and fitted with an image-intensifier night vision system, is mounted in the roof forward of his hatch.

Main armament is a 105 millimeter 52 caliber rifled tank gun designed by OTO Melara. The gun features a falling wedge breech block, concentric buffer, and spring recuperator. During the recoil sequence, the automatic breech-block opens up and ejects the spent cartridge case into a bag located under the breech. The barrel itself has a thermal sleeve and a bore evacuator.

The gun fires all standard 105mm NATO rounds—armor-piercing, discarding sabot; high explosive, antitank; high-explosive squash head; and smoke rounds. A total of 15 rounds are carried in the turret, while an additional 42 rounds are stored in the tank's hull to the left of the driver.

The manufacturer claims that a well-trained crew can fire up to nine rounds per minute. A 7.62mm NATO machine gun is mounted coaxially to the left of the main gun, and a similar machine gun is mounted on the top of the turret for outside use. For concealment, the OF-40 has eight electrically operated smoke dischargers, four mounted on each side of the turret.

While the exact combination and thicknesses of the tank's armor have not been disclosed, it is believed that the OF-40 has less armor than most other MBTs. The tank's side skirts are believed to be made from steel that has been layered and sandwiched between two layers of rubber. International armor experts believe that, in addition to helping to keep the tracks cleaner, the skid design offers some protection against shape-charged antitank weaponry.

At present the OF-40 is also offered in a Mark 2 configuration (not to be confused with the British Mark series). These upgrades are minor in terms of overall design and include a new stabilization system for the main gun and fire-control-system sensors that include wind velocity, powder temperature, ambient temperature, and type of ammunition. Also added is a stabilized panoramic day/night periscope that is directly linked to the gun and can be used for firing.

To date, the United Arab Emirates is the only buyer of the OF-40 tank; it has taken delivery of a total of 36 tanks. But the OF-40 has been tested in Thailand and demonstrated in Egypt. In addition, OTO Melara and Fiat are said to be talking with representatives from Greece and Spain about beginning local production.

If additional buyers can be found for the OF-40, production could resume immediately. Fiat is currently testing a new diesel engine that puts out up to 1,200 horsepower. If the tests are successful, the OF-40

Mark 3 tanks may sport this more powerful engine, which would increase the tank's power-to-weight ratio.

OF-40 Main Battle Tank	
Country:	Italy
Type:	Main Battle Tank
Dimensions	
Length:	6.9 m (22.6 ft)
Width:	3.5 m (11.5 ft)
Height:	2.45 m (8 ft)
Combat weight:	45,500 kg (50.1 tons)
Engine:	Fiat MTU 10 cylinder supercharged diesel
Armament:	One 105mm rifled main gun; two 7.62mm NATO machine guns
Crew:	4
Speed:	60 km/h (37 mph)
Range:	600 km (372 mi)
Obstacle/grade performance:	1.1 m (3.6 ft)
Date of service:	1981

Italian Tanks

Caption for pic 230

Right: The Italian OF-40 somewhat resembles the West German Leopard 1 MBT. Designed and built primarily as an export tank, it is now in service in the United Arab Emirates.

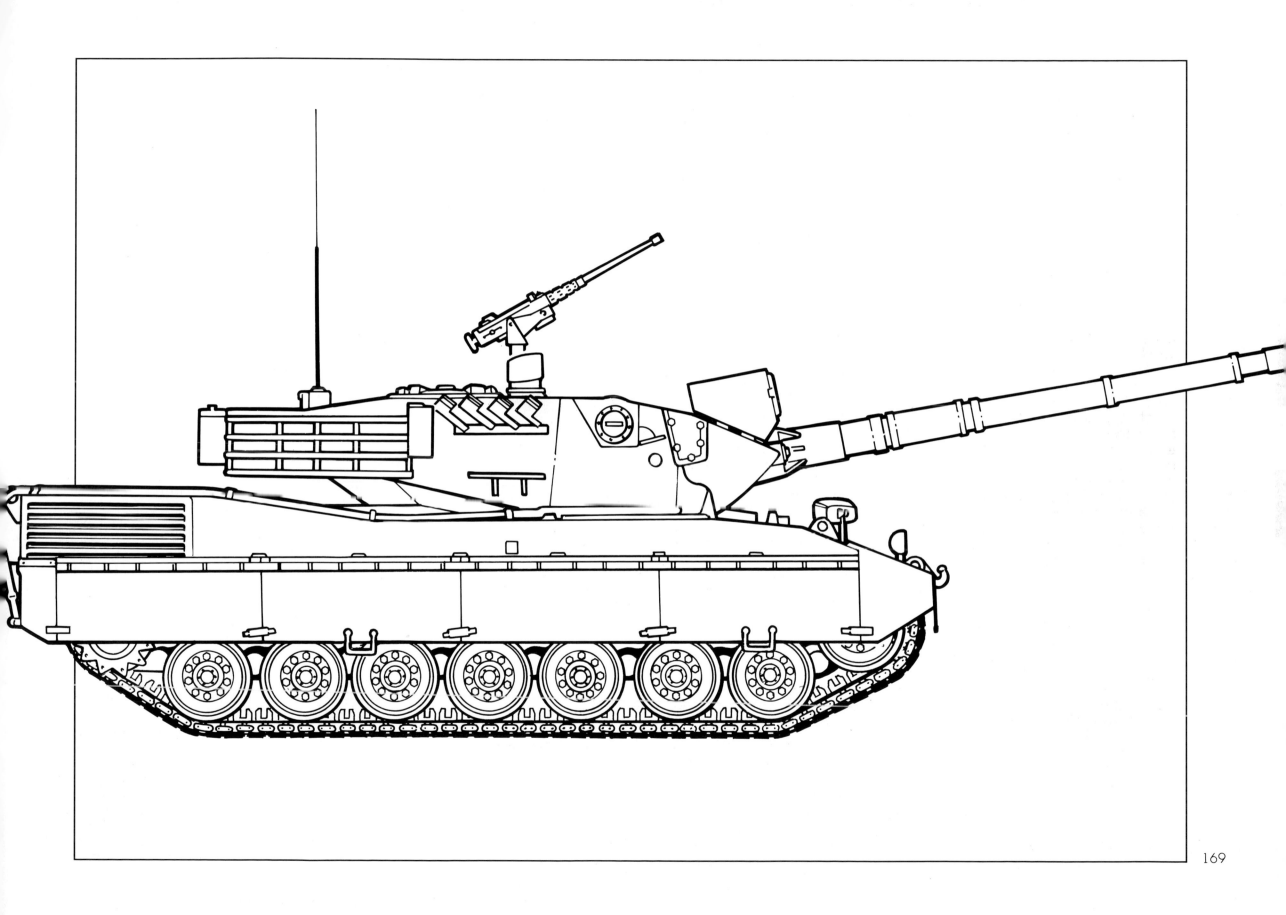

169

C-1 Ariete Main Battle Tank

The Italian C-1 Ariete is the first Italian Main Battle Tank (MBT) design that is contemporary to and comparable with other NATO and Warsaw Pact armored forces. In 1984 the firms of OTO Melara and IVECO Fiat formed a partnership to jointly develop a new MBT and an eight by eight (8-wheeled) tank destroyer for the Italian Army. Out of this partnership has come the C-1 Ariete, or Ram.

According to the agreement between the two companies, IVECO Fiat would be responsible for the various automotive components, while OTO Melara would take charge of weapons and systems development. Together they would develop a design that would fit the indigenous needs of Italy, as well as provide a marketable tank for export sales.

The Ariete tank hull is to be manufactured from welded steel, while the frontal arc of the tank is to sport a new composite armor design that remains classified. Speculation centers on a Chobham design that combines composites, steels, depleted uranium, and laminates. Overall, the design of the tank is contemporary in terms of crew positioning. The commander, gunner, and loader are located in the turret, and the driver sits in the front of the vehicle and utilizes three integral periscopes for viewing. For night driving, the center periscope can easily be replaced with a passive image intensifier. The tank's commander has a rear-opening hatch with observation periscopes.

Main armament is a 120 millimeter smoothbore gun developed by OTO Melara and stabilized on both axes. The tank carries approximately 40 rounds of ammunition that is completely interchangeable with rounds used by American M-1A1 Abrams and German Leopard 2 tanks. The turret has blow-out panels located in its roof for safety from ammunition hits. The ammunition resupply hatch is located on the tank's left side. Supplemental armament includes two

7.62mm NATO machine guns. One is mounted coaxially with the main gun, while the other is located atop the Ariete's turret. For rapid concealment, the tank has eight electrically operated smoke dischargers, four on each side of its turret.

Using a state-of-the-art modular fire control system, the tank features a system called the Officine Galileo TURMS (Tank Universal Reconfigurable Modular System) OG14L3. This system enables computer integration of the commander's day sight, the gunner's periscope laser sight, the ballistic computer, muzzle reference system, on-board sensors, and the control panels of the commander, gunner, and loader. Representing the latest in technology designs, the fire control system is as advanced as any tank on the battlefield today, and it will likely remain so for years to come. Sighting and aiming systems include a stabilized day/night thermal image intensifier, and the latest in laser range finders.

The tank will feature the newly developed Fiat V-12 MTCA diesel engine that is an intercooled, turbocharged 12-cylinder design. The power plant will be coupled with a West German designed ZF transmission and will feature four forward gears and two reverse gears. The tank moves on a pair of seven rubber-tire road wheels, an idler at the front, a drive sprocket, and track return rollers.

A total of six prototype tanks have been built so far and are undergoing extensive testing with the Italian Army. It is anticipated that sometime during 1989 the Italian government will place orders for as many as 300 Ariete C-1 tanks. Upon delivery of the first units, which is expected in 1991, the vast majority of the new tanks will replace aging M-60A1 tanks that are currently deployed in three armored brigades guarding the Gorizia Gap on the Yugoslavian border. The M-60A1 tanks will then be used to replace those Italian units that are still using the venerable M-

47 tanks of post-World War II vintage. A simplified and less sophisticated export version could be available for the world marketplace as early as 1992.

C-1 Ariete Main Battle Tank	
Country:	Italy
Type:	Main Battle Tank
Dimensions	
Length:	7.6 m (24.9 ft)
Width:	3.6 m (11.8 ft)
Height:	2.5 m (8.2 ft)
Combat weight:	48,000 kg (52.9 tons)
Engine:	Fiat V-12 MTCA intercooled turbocharged V-12 diesel
Armament:	One 120mm smoothbore main gun; two 7.62mm NATO machine guns
Crew:	4
Speed:	65+ km/h (40+mph)
Range:	550+ km (341+ mi)
Obstacle/grade performance:	Undisclosed
Date of service:	1990

Right: The C-1 Ariete is the new Italian Main Battle Tank and will be built and used by Italy and Spain. It entered production in 1989. At least 200 Ariete MBTs will be built.

Type 95 KE-GO Light Tank

Perhaps the most ubiquitous of all Imperial Japanese tanks was the Type 95. The Type 89 was originally intended to be a light tank, but armor and the 57 millimeter gun raised it into the medium class and made it very slow. Therefore, in 1933 design work began on a new tank that could keep up with the newly formed mechanized infantry.

Nearly 1,250 of these light tanks were built by Mitsubishi and others under the name of HA-GO (the military designation was KE-GO) between 1935 and 1942. They were used in both cavalry and infantry roles on every front in the Great East Asian War.

The Type 95 was powered by an improved air-cooled diesel engine, which was built by Mitsubishi and which produced 120 horsepower. The hull was of iron girder construction, suitably reinforced and covered with armor to a maximum thickness of .47 inch. Woven asbestos curtains lined the interior to protect the three crewmembers—driver, machine gunner, and tank commander—from heat thrown off by the air-cooled engine. The curtain also served as a cushion when traversing rough ground. Space between the curtain and the hull wall supposedly allowed air to circulate. The driver sat on the right side in the front behind a hatch that could be propped open. The machine gunner sat to the driver's left, and the tank commander sat, or stood, in the turret.

The Type 95 was armed with a 37mm main gun as well as two Type 91 6.5mm machine guns, one mounted in the hull and the other in the turret facing to the rear. The 6.5mm machine guns were exchanged for more powerful 7.7mm Type 97 machine guns in 1941. The commander was responsible for loading, aiming, and firing the main gun. The Type 95 tank carried two types of ammunition, Type 94 high-explosive and Type 94 armor-piercing.

The most characteristic feature of the Type 95 was its simple suspension system. The tracks were driven through the front sprocket. Two bogie wheels were suspended on a single bell crank with two bell cranks per side. There were two return wheels. For all its ruggedness and simple maintenance, the suspension system had a tendency to pitch so badly on rough ground that the crew sometimes found it impossible to drive at any speed. In the close confines of the hull, motion sickness was often a problem.

The Type 95 was modified more than any other Japanese tank. In 1943 Type 95s were equipped with a 57mm gun and redesignated the Type 3 KE-RI. The following year, more Type 95s were modified by adding the turret used on the Type 97 medium tank and a 47mm gun; it was redesignated the Type 4 KE-NU. An amphibious version, the Type 2 KA-MI, was also built. It carried a fourth crewmember, responsible for amphibious preparations and two detachable pontoons. This amphibious version was used primarily by Special Naval Landing Forces, but by the time it entered service, most Japanese amphibious landing operations were over. The Type 2 KA-MI was encountered by the United States Marines and Army in the Marshall and Mariana islands, particularly on Guam, where it was used—and largely wasted—in static defense positions.

A final modification, designated the Type 98 KE-NI, traveled at 31 miles per hour and was somewhat lighter than the original Type 95, even with its heavier (.62 inch) armor. It entered production in 1942, but only about 200 were manufactured.

Like the Type 89, the Type 95 and its variants were used in all theaters of the Great East Asian War, primarily to support infantry or as cavalry reconnaissance and, to a lesser extent, as raiding vehicles. When the war ended in August 1945, hundreds of Type 95s were left in China. They were reportedly used by the army of the People's Republic of China during the Korean War.

Type 95 KE-GO Light Tank and variants	
Country:	Imperial Japan
Type:	Light Tank
Dimensions Length: Width: Height:	4.38 m (14.4 ft) 2.06 m (6.75 ft) 2.49 m (8.2 ft)
Combat weight:	6,804 kg (7.5 tons)
Engine:	Mitsubishi 6 cylinder air-cooled diesel
Armament:	One 37mm Type 94 main gun; two 6.5mm Type 91 machine guns, replaced by two 7.7mm Type 97 machine guns after 1941
Crew:	3
Speed:	45 km/h (28 mph)
Range:	250 km (155 mi)
Obstacle/grade performance:	0.8 m (2.6 ft)
Date of service:	1935

Right: The Japanese Type 95 Light Tank was equipped with a 37mm main gun. Many Type 95s ended up as stationary pillboxes resisting American landing forces during the Pacific islands campaign. **Far right:** The Type 95 was designed to accompany mechanized infantry forces.

Type 97 SHINHOTO CHI-HA Medium Tank

Japanese Army observers watched tank developments in Europe and studied as avidly as any European military officer the operational experiences gained by German, Soviet, and Italian tanks in the Spanish Civil War (1936–39). What they saw and reported convinced Army Technical Headquarters that the Type 89 medium tank was too lightly armored and gunned to meet Western tanks on an equal basis. A heavier, faster tank with strengthened armor was needed to provide long-range fire support for the Type 95 Light Tank and the new mechanized brigades.

In 1937 two prototypes—one designed by the General Staff, the other designed by the engineering department of Army Technical Headquarters—were tested. Although the General Staff design was cheaper to produce, the outbreak of war with China that same year eliminated economy as a concern. The design by Army Technical Headquarters won and was put into production the following year. The winning design, built by Mitsubishi and designated the CHI-HA, used the Mitsubishi air-cooled diesel engine now up-rated to 170 horsepower. The Type 97, as finally approved, used the same reinforced-girder construction as the Type 95 Light Tank. Armor plate was considerably thicker than the Type 95.

The Type 97 mounted a short-barrel 57 millimeter Type 90 gun and two 7.7mm machine guns and carried a crew of four. The tank commander and the gunner sat in the turret. With the gunner in the turret also, the tank commander was relieved of the multiple duties of having to command the tank; act as observer, machine gunner, and loader; and lay and fire the main gun. The driver sat in the front right-hand side of the hull, the machine gunner the front left-hand side.

The suspension system was similar to that used in the Type 95 but was considerably stronger. Six bogie wheels per side were mounted on bell cranks: four wheels on each side in two independent pairs of bell cranks and the fore and aft bogie wheels on separate bell cranks. All were supported by resisting springs encased in armored tubes. Three return wheels, carried the track on top. The center roller bore only the inside half of the track, while the other two supported the track along its full width. The tracks were driven from a front driving sprocket by a drive shaft that ran through a tunnel in the hull from the rear-mounted engine to a gearbox.

The Type 97 received its combat baptism in Manchuria and against Soviet forces on the Mongolian border in May through September of 1939. Post-battle analysis showed that the CHI-HA was handicapped by its low-velocity gun when dealing with enemy tanks. A new turret mounting a more powerful high-velocity, long-barrel 47mm semiautomatic gun of 48 caliber was designed and tested. But the new turret and main gun were not put into production until 1942. Complacency after easy victories in China and Manchuria, as well as the conquests of Vietnam, Malaya, Burma, and the Dutch East Indies, caused the delay.

When the Type 97 entered service, properly equipped and supported mechanized infantry units were realized. The skill with which Japanese commanders maneuvered their mechanized infantry divisions was best seen in Malaya. Japanese units moved so fast, and were so heavily supported by armor, that British defenders never had a chance to establish effective defense lines.

A number of variations of the Type 97 were produced with more powerful engines and heavier armor. The Type 1 CHI-NE had 2 inches of armor and a 240 horsepower air-cooled diesel engine. The Type 3 CHI-NU was equipped with a new turret and a 75mm gun. The Type 4 CHI-TO had a longer hull, weighed 30 tons, and carried a 75mm 38 caliber gun. The last variation, the Type 5, weighed 37 tons and was armed with a 75mm main gun and a secondary 37mm gun. It carried 3 inches of armor and would have been superior to the American M-4 Sherman. The war ended before it could be built.

The Type 97 SHINHOTO CHI-HA served against Allied forces throughout the Pacific and east Asia and against the Soviets during the July–August 1945 Lightning War in Manchuria. Its 47mm gun could almost penetrate M-4 Sherman armor.

Type 97 SHINHOTO CHI-HA Medium Tank and variants

Country:	Imperial Japan
Type:	Medium Tank
Dimensions	
Length:	5.51 m (18 ft)
Width:	2.33 m (7.6 ft)
Height:	2.23 m (7.3 ft)
Combat weight:	15,000 kg (16.5 tons)
Engine:	Mitsubishi 12 cylinder air-cooled diesel
Armament:	One 57mm Type 90 main gun, later up-gunned to 47mm 48 caliber; two 7.7mm Type 97 machine guns
Crew:	4
Speed:	38 km/h (23.5 mph)
Range:	210 km (130 mi)
Obstacle/grade performance:	0.8 m (2.6 ft)
Date of service:	1938

Right: The Japanese Type 97 Medium Tank was intended to replace the slower, more lightly armed Type 89. **Far right:** The Type 97 was distributed in three or four companies per armored regiment. Each company was made up of three platoons containing three tanks each. Three to five additional Type 97s were attached to regimental headquarters.

Type 61 Main Battle Tank

In 1950, five years after the end of World War II, Japan began to rearm. The threat motivating rearmament in a country severely shocked by the loss of the Great East Asian War was the traditional threat from the west, the Soviet Union. The terms and conditions of rearmament, however, were far different from those of the period 1870 to 1945, when Japan had lifted itself by its bootstraps from a backward, non-technical nation to a major world power with imperial ambitions. Now rearmament was directed toward defensive rather than offensive operations.

At first, the United States supplied M-4 Shermans and M-24 Chaffees to the new Japanese Self Defense Forces. These were soon considered obsolete and too heavy. Consequently, the Japanese Self Defense Forces sought a light—less than 40 tons—and highly mobile tank. They also wanted a tank that could be built in Japan to help revive the country's shattered industrial base. The first design, the STA-1, and its three predecessors emphasized these qualities and were even light-

178

er than the Swiss 36.5 ton Panzer 61, a medium tank mounting a 105 millimeter main gun.

The STA-3 design was adopted, and production of the Type 61 tank began in 1961. Initially, it weighed 34.5 tons and mounted a 90mm main gun similar to that used on the American M-48 Patton. A total of 564 Type 61s are believed to have been produced, but actual production figures are classified. In its final configuration, the Type 61 weighed 38.5 tons.

The Type 61's engine was built by Mitsubishi-Nippon Heavy Industries, Ltd., which was reorganized and renamed after the war. The V-12 air-cooled diesel engine displaced 29.6 liters and produced 600 horsepower. This engine continued the Japanese practice of mounting air-cooled diesel engines in armored vehicles, a practice that began in 1934 with the Type 89B Medium Tank.

The Type 61's design is conventional. The hull is of welded construction and is divided into three compartments, driving in the front, fighting in the center, and engine in the rear. The commander and gunner sit in the turret on the right, the loader in the turret on the left. The driver sits in the front of the hull on the right-hand side. The turret is cast in one piece and resembles the American M-47 with its large overhanging bustle. Armor is rather light for a Main Battle Tank: only 2.5 inches maximum on the turret face, 1.8 inches on the glacis down to a minimum of .6 inch on the hull rear.

The 90mm gun is fitted with a T-style muzzle brake and a fume extractor to keep breech gases out of the tank. The gun fires armor-piercing capped and high-explosive ammunition. Secondary armament is based on the American pattern: A 7.62mm NATO machine gun mounted coaxially with the main gun and a .50 caliber machine gun mounted on the turret top for antiaircraft use. No nuclear-bio-

logical-chemical (NBC) protection is fitted, although there is provision for storing NBC protective clothing and respirators.

An armored bridge-laying vehicle (Type 67), armored engineer vehicle (Type 67), armored recovery vehicle (Type 70), and a Type 61 training tank have also been designed and built. The Type 61 tank was never exported.

Type 61 Main Battle Tank and variants	
Country:	Japan
Type:	Main Battle Tank
Dimensions	
Length:	6.3 m (20.6 ft)
Width:	2.95 m (9.7 ft)
Height:	2.95 m (9.7 ft)
Combat weight:	35,000 kg (38.6 tons)
Engine:	Mitsubishi Type 12, 12 cylinder air-cooled diesel
Armament:	One 90mm Type 61 main gun; one 7.62mm NATO Browning M1919A4 machine gun; one 12.5mm .50 caliber Browning M2 HB machine gun
Crew:	4
Speed:	45 km/h (28 mph)
Range:	200 km (124 mi)
Obstacle/grade performance:	0.7 m (2.3 ft)
Date of service:	1961

Left: The Type 61 Main Battle Tank was the first armored vehicle designed and built in post-war Japan. A total of 559 Type 61 MBTs were built. The Type 61 shown here has the turret traversed to the rear. **Right:** The Type 74 Main Battle Tank began to supplement and replace the Type 61 in September 1975. A total of 850 Type 74s were manufactured.

Almost as soon as the Type 61 Main Battle Tank (MBT) was approved for production in 1961, design work began on a new MBT for the Japanese Self Defense Forces. The new MBT was to be capable of meeting the Soviet MBT threat expected through the 1980s—the T-55, T-64, T-72 tanks.

Various configurations and prototypes were tested between 1962 and 1971 before the STB-3 design was chosen in 1974. Earlier prototypes tested such new components as the hydropneumatic suspension from the American–West German MBT 70 design, the German Leopard 1 hull, and the French AMX-30 turret. Even an automatic loader from the British-designed L7A1 105 millimeter main gun had been tested before being dropped as too complicated and expensive.

The hull of the Type 74 MBT, like that of the Type 61, is of conventional welded construction and divided into three compartments, driving in the front, fighting in the center, and the engine compartment at the rear. Crew disposition is nearly the same as for the Type 61: The commander and gunner are seated in the turret on the right side, the loader in the turret on the left. The difference is the driver, who sits in the front of the hull on the left-hand side. When buttoned up, the driver uses three periscopes, one of which is infrared.

The commander's station is equipped with similar periscopes with infrared capability. Armor is considerably thicker than on the Type 61, but exact composition and dimensions are classified.

Mitsubishi designed a new 750 horsepower, ten cylinder air-cooled diesel engine for the Type 74. It drives the MBT at a published speed of 33 miles per hour, although *Jane's Armour Artillery* has reported it can reach speeds of 37 miles per hour or faster. The hydropneumatic suspension system was adopted in modified form; it can raise or lower the tank to give additional ground or head clearance up to a maximum of 2.31 inches. The suspension system can also tilt the tank to provide additional travel for the main gun or provide a stable platform for calculating main gun trajectories.

The Type 74's main gun is the British Royal Ordnance L7, manufactured in Japan. It fires the standard range of ammunition suitable for this gun plus armor-piercing, discarding sabot-tracer and high-explosive, squash head-tracer. A Nippon Electric laser range finder provides range information to the commander and to the gunner's fire control computer. Secondary armament consists of a 7.62mm Type 74 machine gun mounted coaxially with the main gun and a Browning M2 HB on a pintle mount between the commander's and loader's cupolas, where either can reach it. A white/infrared searchlight and infrared driving lights are also standard equipment. Three smoke dischargers are mounted on either side of the turret, but the tank mounts no grenade launchers.

The Type 74 has been the MBT of the Japanese Self Defense Forces for the 1980s. It is supported by a lesser number of Type 61 MBTs. Both tanks are distributed through a single armored division (the 7th), twelve infantry divisions, two composite brigades, five engineer brigades, and one each of airborne, artillery, and signal brigades. The tank division and each of the infantry divisions contain one tank battalion. Each tank battalion contains 60 tanks.

The Type 74 entered service in 1974, and an estimated 850 Type 74s were built. Exact figures are classified. The Type 78 Armored Recovery Vehicle is the only known variant. Like the Type 61, the Type 74 MBT has never been exported.

Type 74 Main Battle Tank	
Country:	Japan
Type:	Main Battle Tank
Dimensions	
Length:	7.84 m (25.7 ft)
Width:	3.18 m (10 4 ft)
Height:	2.48 m (8.1 ft)
Combat weight:	38,000 kg (41.9 tons)
Engine:	Mitsubishi Type 22, 10 cylinder air-cooled diesel
Armament:	One 105mm Type 74 main gun; one 7.62mm NATO Type 74 machine gun; one 12.5mm .50 caliber Browning M2 HB machine gun
Crew:	4
Speed:	53 km/h (33 mph), nominal
Range:	300 km (186 mi)
Obstacle/grade performance:	1.0 m (3.28 ft)
Date of service:	1974

Type 59 Main Battle Tank

In the early 1950s the Soviet Union provided the People's Republic of China with a supply of their then state-of-the-art T-54 Main Battle Tank (MBT). Within a few years, the Chinese had dissected the T-54 and were producing their own "homegrown" version that they called the Type 59 or T-59. Early production models were nearly identical to the Soviet T-54.

Easily recognized by its large, squatty, dome-shaped turret and the giant gap between its first and second road wheels, the Type 59 MBT has undergone a host of changes, modifications, and retrofits since first being "reverse engineered" by

the Chinese in the 1950s. Originally equipped with the Soviet-designed 100 millimeter D-10 gun, the Chinese developed an armor-piercing, fin-stabilized, discarding sabot projectile, designated the AP-100/2. The round has a long rod penetrator and saddle-type sabot with eight stabilizing fins that can penetrate the armor of today's more modern vehicles. The casing of the round is semicombustible (it burns up after firing while still in the barrel) so that all that is left of the round is the stubby end of the casing, which ejects when the breech is opened. It is believed the Type 59 can carry 34 rounds of ammunition. In 1987 a later ver-

sion was seen equipped with what is believed to be a modified 105mm rifled gun that is fitted with a normal fume extractor and thermal sleeve. This up-gunning of the Type 59 is significant and will be of interest to a host of international companies seeking to retrofit these aging armored vehicles.

Basic in its technology, the Type 59 tank has sported a variety of new equipment over its long history. Soon after entering production, Chinese engineers added fume extractors and infrared night vision equipment. Today, many Western nations are offering retrofit and modernization

Left: The Chinese Type 59 Main Battle Tank is armed with a 100mm main gun and one 12.7mm and two 7.62mm machine guns. **Right:** The Type 59 is essentially a domestic version of the Soviet T-54. This Type 59 was sold to Pakistan, where it has been refitted with the British 105mm L7 main gun.

programs for the Type 59 MBT. Some of the most recent additions have centered on equipping the tank commander and the gunner each with his own large infrared searchlight. The searchlights are located above the 100mm main gun and move in elevation with it. In addition, it is believed that some Type 59 tanks have been outfitted with laser range finders that are located to the right of the infrared searchlights. While much of the technology made available to the Chinese is not openly discussed, several British companies have supplied the Chinese with passive night vision equipment that includes image intensifier periscopes for the gunner, the driver, and the commander.

At present, it is believed that the Chinese Type 59 tank is no longer in production,

but it is certain to remain in service with nearly a dozen nations for many years to come. Production began in 1957 at the Baotou military plant in the Beijing military district, and it is estimated that throughout the 1970s between 500 and 700 Type 59 tanks rolled off the assembly lines each year. By 1979 Chinese production may have risen to as high as 1,000 tanks per year. While no exact production figures are available, it is believed that thousands of Type 59 tanks have been produced.

The Chinese company known as NORINCO (Chinese North Industries Corporation) has announced a retrofit program for the Type 59. The company is offering to replace the rather limited 520 horsepower diesel engine with a new 730 horsepower version that would greatly

increase the tank's power-to-weight ratio. Other modifications include a rubber coating inside the tracks for a quieter ride, an inexpensive nuclear-biological-chemical protection system, a new stabilizer system for the main gun in both elevation and traverse modes, and a new fire control system for the gunner's sight.

Type 59 Main Battle Tank

Country:	China
Type:	Main Battle Tank
Dimensions	
Length:	6.04 m (19.8 ft)
Width:	3.27 m (10.7 ft)
Height:	2.59 m (8.5 ft)
Combat weight:	36,000 kg (39.7 tons)
Engine:	Model 12150L V-12 water-cooled diesel
Armament:	One 100mm rifled main gun; one 7.62mm machine gun
Crew:	4
Speed:	40–50 km/h (25–31 mph)
Range:	420–440 km (260–273 mi)
Obstacle/grade performance:	0.79 m (2.6 ft)
Date of service:	Late 1950s

Left: More than 3,600 Chinese Type 59 MBTs have been manufactured since the tank entered service in the late 1950s. More than 11 nations have purchased the Type 59 from the People's Republic of China. **Right:** The People's Republic of China supplied Type 59s to North Vietnam. This Type 59 was captured by South Vietnamese forces in 1972.

183

Type 69 Main Battle Tank

When it comes to Chinese tank design, the byword seems to be evolutionary rather than revolutionary. Such appears to be the case with the People's Republic of China's Type 69 Main Battle Tank, which some sources say has been in production since 1969. Although first seen during a military parade near Beijing in 1982, many believe that the Type 69 was developed much earlier and is based upon the same hull, turret, and chassis as the earlier Type 59.

Informed military sources at the Pentagon believe that, while the Type 69 may have been around since the late 1960s, it did not enter full production until the late 1970s or early 1980s. The tank itself isn't much more than an upgraded version of earlier Chinese tank technology. It also appears that the Type 69-I tank began production with a smoothbore 100 millimeter gun, but after a relatively short period of "after-production" testing, a rifled 100mm gun found on older tank models proved to be more effective and accurate. It is now believed that the smoothbore gun has been dropped completely from production in favor of the rifled version, even though nearly 200 of the smoothbore version were delivered to Iraq with Saudi Arabia acting as the middleman arms merchant.

While very similar to the older Type 59 Chinese tank, the newer Type 69-II not only appears to have the more reliable rifled gun but also sports a host of improvements and refinements that add to the tank's protective armament, fire control system, and night detection/imaging. With its rifled gun, it is believed that the Type 69 tank can fire all types of ammunition—including high-explosive, antitank; high-explosive; armor-piercing; and armor-piercing, fin-stabilized, discarding sabot rounds.

The Type 69-II has a main gun that is stabilized on both axes and sports a simplified fire control system for increased accuracy. This system comprises a ballistic computer, a laser range finder, and the gun sight. The range finder measures the distance to the target, and this information is automatically fed into the computer. The computer then feeds its computations to the automatic range-setting system and the gun control mechanism, where the elevation is set. Two versions have been seen on the Type 69 tanks. The first has the laser range finder located atop the main gun, where it appears to be extremely vulnerable to small arms fire and shell fragments. The other system appears to be located inside the tank turret itself for additional protection.

In addition to the 100mm main gun, the Type 69 has a 12.7mm Type 54 antiaircraft machine gun located on the outside of the turret near the tank loader's cupola. Two additional 7.62mm Type 59T machine guns are also found on the tank. One machine gun is coaxially mounted by the main gun, the other is located down below the tank's headlights on the bow of the hull.

In addition to being in service with the People's Republic of China Army, the Type 69 is currently in service in Iraq and Thailand. Variants include a Type 69 bridge layer, a variant with 57mm antiaircraft guns, and a tank recovery vehicle for picking up and retrieving tanks that have either broken down or are knocked out of commission. The Type 69 tank is believed to still be in limited production, but it is likely to be phased out as the more technologically advanced Type 80 tank begins production.

184

Type 69 Main Battle Tank	
Country:	China
Type:	Main Battle Tank
Dimensions	
Length:	6.24 m (20.5 ft)
Width:	3.29 m (10.8 ft)
Height:	2.8 m (9.2 ft)
Combat weight:	36,500–37,000 kg (40.2–40.8 tons)
Engine:	Type 12150L-7BW V-12 diesel
Armament:	**Type I:** one 100mm smoothbore main gun **Type II:** one 100mm rifled main gun **Types I and II:** one 12.7mm antiaircraft machine gun; two 7.62mm machine guns
Crew:	4
Speed:	50 km/h (31 mph)
Range:	420–440 km (260–273 mi)
Obstacle/grade performance:	0.8 m (2.6 ft)
Date of service:	Early 1980s (estimated)

Type 80 Main Battle Tank

First seen in 1985 when it was called the Type 69-III by the Chinese, this new tank was later renamed the Type 80 and appears to be an evolutionary change to a new design that features a new chassis, is up-gunned, and carries a turret very similar to the earlier Type 69s.

The tank itself is of an all-welded steel construction and features a conventional layout: The driver up front on the left side, the turret in the center, and the power train in the rear. The commander sits in the turret on the left side; the gunner is forward and below the commander; the loader is positioned on the right. It appears that a host of periscopes are provided for the crew to view and observe their surroundings when buttoned up, and the driver has either two day scopes or one day/night scope for maneuvering after dark.

Up-gunned from previous Chinese tanks, the new Type 80 sports a 105 millimeter rifled gun that is reportedly very similar in appearance to the West's L7/M68. How the Chinese secured this technology is unknown, but many now speculate that they reverse engineered the gun system and have a variant that is capable of firing both Chinese- and Western-made ammunition, including high-explosive, anti-tank; high-explosive squash head; and armor-piercing, fin-stabilized, discarding sabot rounds. The gun is capable of slewing through a complete 360° circle and has powered elevation from −4° up to a maximum elevation of +18° The gun itself is complete with a Western-type fume extractor system and thermal heat sleeve.

In addition to the main gun, there is a 12.7mm antiaircraft machine gun located externally near the loader's hatch and a 7.62mm machine gun coaxially mounted with the 105mm main gun. For concealment, the tank also mounts a total of eight forward-firing, electrically operated smoke dischargers, four on each

side of the turret. There is a metal storage basket that runs around the sides and rear portion of the turret for carrying additional supplies and equipment.

The tank sports a sophisticated laser range finder, ballistic computer, stabilized sights, gun stabilized on both axes, and an image-stabilized fire control system. The system enables the Type 80 tank to engage and fire on either moving or stationary targets while the tank itself moves and maneuvers on the road or cross-country.

The tank has a newly designed nuclear-biological-chemical protection system and comes with armor-protected side skirts. Up front the Type 80 has been designed so that additional panels of composite armor can be added to the frontal arc region as threats develop or increase.

To extend the tank's range, two large drum fuel tanks can be mounted at the rear and quickly jettisoned when empty or when the tank goes into combat maneuvers.

The Type 80 is equipped with six rubber-tire road wheels on each side of the tank, with the idler at the front and the drive sprocket at the rear. A new suspension system using a torsion bar and hydraulic shock absorbers is also being used. The power plant is believed to be a turbocharged version of the Type 12150L-7BW diesel engine that is used on the earlier Type 69 tank.

It is believed that development of the Type 80 Main Battle Tank (MBT) is now complete but that the tank has not yet gone into full-scale production. Some believe that while the Chinese have a need for a new MBT for its own army, they are awaiting orders from foreign marketplaces before committing to adoption of the new vehicle design.

Type 80 Main Battle Tank	
Country:	China
Type:	Main Battle Tank
Dimensions	
Length:	6.32 m (20.7 ft)
Width:	3.37 m (11 ft)
Height:	2.87 m (9.4 ft)
Combat weight:	38,000 kg (41.9 tons)
Engine:	Type 12150L-7BW turbocharged V-12 diesel
Armament:	One 105mm rifled main gun; one 12.7mm antiaircraft machine gun; one 7.62mm machine gun
Crew:	4
Speed:	57–60 km/h (35–37 mph)
Range:	430 km (266 mi)
Obstacle/grade performance:	0.8 m (2.6 ft)
Date of service:	First seen, 1985; ready for full production

SOUTH KOREA
Type 88 ROKIT Main Battle Tank

The Type 88 ROKIT Main Battle Tank is the first homegrown tank South Korea has produced. Known originally as the XK-1 Republic of Korea Indigenous Tank, or ROKIT, the vehicle prototypes reflect a combination of Korean design talents and expertise supplied by the Land Systems Division of General Dynamics.

The first prototype tested the automotive performance of the new tank design and was called the Automotive Test Rig when it was delivered to Aberdeen Proving Grounds, Maryland, in November 1983. In essence, the first prototype was what is termed a "fully payloaded" tank; it was fitted with nonoperating elements, such as the turret, but reflected the full weight and balance of the tank. The second prototype was called the Fire Control Test Rig, and it was delivered to Aberdeen in February 1984 to undergo extensive fire control tests.

Externally, the Type 88 tank bears a strong resemblance to the American M-1A1 Abrams, although the ROKIT weighs less, has one less road wheel per side, and has a slightly lower silhouette to meet the needs of survivability in the Korean terrain. The "look-alike" influence from General Dynamics, the makers of the M-1A1, is obvious, but the ROKIT features advanced components and systems not found on the American tank.

In terms of the operating layout, the driver is located up front on the left side. In the turret, the commander is located on the right side, the gunner below and forward of the commander, and the loader on the left side.

The main gun for the ROKIT is the American-designed M68A1 105 millimeter rifled tank gun, which is currently in use on many older South Korean M-48A5 tanks. The barrel itself has a fume extractor, thermal heat sleeve, and a muzzle reference system. Mounted coaxially with the main gun is a 7.62mm machine gun, and

there is a 7.62mm machine gun by the loader's hatch. A 12.7mm antiaircraft machine gun is mounted on the roof of the turret. The tank has a total of 12 electrically operated smoke dischargers for concealment, six on each side of the turret.

In terms of the fire control system, the ROKIT features state-of-the-art components that use both American- and French-designed systems. High-technology ballistic computers, laser range finders, sensors to compensate for crosswinds, and two-axes-stabilized day/night sighting systems enable the tank to engage both moving and stationary targets while it is itself traveling either on the road or across open terrain. One of the most unusual features of the Type 88 tank is a hybrid suspension system that uses hydropneumatic units to allow the tank to figuratively kneel. Not only does this reduce the tank's profile but it also enables the gun to be depressed to -10° for firing downhill at a more severe angle.

The Type 88 tank has six rubber-tire road wheels on each side, with the idler at the front and the drive sprocket at the rear. A diesel engine mates to an automatic transmission with four forward speeds and two reverse gears. The tank provides nuclear-biological-chemical protection with gas particular filters and a full fire detection/suppression system.

Production of the Type 88 tank began in 1985, and the first of several battalions was equipped with the new tank in the fall of 1987. It is expected that the South Korean army will eventually take delivery of more than 700 Type 88 tanks. A simplified export version is being readied for sale by the early 1990s.

Type 88 ROKIT Main Battle Tank	
Country:	Republic of South Korea
Type:	Main Battle Tank
Dimensions	
Length:	7.47 m (24.5 ft)
Width:	3.59 m (11.8 ft)
Height:	2.24 m (7.3 ft)
Combat weight:	51,000 kg (56.2 tons)
Engine:	MTU 871 Ka-501 diesel
Armament:	One 105mm rifled main gun; two 7.62mm machine guns; one 12.7mm antiaircraft machine gun
Crew:	4
Speed:	65 km/h (40 mph)
Range:	500 km (310 mi)
Obstacle/grade performance:	1 m (3.28 ft)
Date of service:	1987

Right: In certain respects, the South Korean Type 88 ROKIT Main Battle Tank is a smaller, lighter version of the American M-1 Abrams. The Type 88 entered production in 1985, and some 700 are expected to be built. The Type 88 is thought to be superior to North Korea's copy of the Soviet T-62.

Glossary

APDS: Armor-piercing, discarding sabot.

APFSDS: Armor-piercing, fin-stabilized, discarding sabot.

Appliqué armor: Additional armor protection usually applied in sheets over existing armor.

Armor-piercing ammunition: Rounds capable of penetrating tank armor. The types of rounds vary; different rounds are effective against different armor. Penetrating ability also depends on distance.

Bi-metallic plate: Armor having two different metals bonded together.

Bogie wheels: See **Road wheels**.

Bore evacuator: System for drawing propellant fumes out of an armored vehicle's gun bore after firing. This prevents the crew compartments from filling with fumes when the breech is opened.

Breech: The rear opening of the tank's main gun where ammunition is loaded.

Bustle: The rearward projection at the back of the tank's turret. The bustle enlarges the interior of the turret, allowing room for additional equipment or ammunition.

Caliber: A measurement of the size of a gun, obtained by dividing the length of the barrel by the diameter of the bore. The higher the caliber, the more powerful the gun.

Canister: Antipersonnel rounds usually consisting of hundreds of small metal balls.

Cartridge case: Container for a tank's ammunition—usually consisting of primer, charge, and projectile.

Chobham armor: Type of ceramic and steel composite armor developed at Chobham, England. This or similar armor is used on most modern tanks.

Coaxial: Usually a machine gun or lighter caliber gun mounted in the same plane and axis as the main gun.

Cruiser tank: A fast, lightly armored, heavily gunned tank that attacks enemy armored forces.

Cupola: Small structure built on top of an armored vehicle's turret. It is usually for the tank commander, less often for another crewmember such as the loader. The cupola may or may not revolve or have its own armament.

Depleted uranium (DU): Nonradioactive metal much denser than steel and used to make penetrator rods and armor.

Discarding sabot (DS): Small-diameter warhead surrounded by metal or plastic jacket of a larger diameter that allows the warhead to be accelerated to a greater speed by a larger gun. The jacket falls away after the warhead leaves the muzzle.

Drive wheels: Wheels, or sprockets, geared to the engine through the transmission and axles and supplying the motive power that turns the tank tread.

Electronic countermeasures (ECM): Used to blind tank movement from enemy radar or other means of electronic detection.

Fin-stabilized (FS) ammunition: Tank round that uses pop-up fins to make the round fly straight. Usually applied to warheads fired from **smoothbore** guns.

Fire control system (FCS): Combination of range finder, computer, and loading device that together form the machinery that aims and fires a tank's main gun.

Fragmentation warhead: Ammunition manufactured so that it breaks up into hundreds of small pieces upon detonation or impact.

Fully payloaded tank: Prototype tank that represents the full weight and balance of a tank design but without the more sophisticated electronic, computer, or infrared equipment common in modern tanks. Used to test chassis, suspension, and hull of a tank design.

Fume extractor: See **Bore extractor**.

Future Soviet Tank (FST): The follow-on generation of Soviet Main Battle Tanks after the T-80. To be deployed in the 1990s.

Glacis: The heavily armored front slope of a tank from the turret to the chassis.

Gyrostabilizer: Device to stabilize a tank's main gun on the vertical and horizontal axes. Enables the gun to be fired accurately while the tank is moving.

Heavy tank: Now obsolete class of heavily gunned and armored tank. Usually quite slow, it supported medium tanks by using long-range antitank fire against enemy armor and antitank weapons.

High-explosive (HE): A substance that oxidizes, or burns, rapidly, producing a large volume of gas with great disruptive effect.

High-explosive, antitank (HEAT) ammunition: Warhead that forms a gas jet that burns through armor.

High-explosive, squash head (HESH) ammunition: High-explosive warhead that flattens on impact across a large area of armor before detonating.

Hull down: A defense position where a tank sits stationary in a ditch.

Idler wheels: Wheels at the opposite end of the tank track from the driving wheels. Idler wheels guide the track in its return path to the drive wheels.

Incendiary ammunition: Warhead containing flammable material.

Infantry tank: A slow moving, heavily armored, lightly gunned tank that supports infantry forces.

Infrared: Pertaining to wavelengths not visible to the human eye. Infrared wavelength permits detection of heat sources, aiding crewmembers in seeing at night or in smoke or fog.

Intercooler: Device for cooling the air used in a combustion engine, allowing the engine to provide more power.

Right: American M-60 Main Battle Tank. Side view shows six road wheels on the bottom, drive wheel in front, idler wheel at rear, and three return roller wheels on top.

Lands: Raised, curved ridges in a gun barrel that provide spin to a projectile.

Laser range finder: A measuring device that uses a laser to illuminate a distant target. A sensor measures the reflected illumination to determine the distance to the target.

Lay: To aim a gun as to direction and elevation before firing.

Light tank: Now obsolete class of lightly armored, lightly gunned, fast tanks used for reconnaissance and close infantry support.

Loader: Crewmember responsible for loading a tank's main gun before firing and unloading the gun after firing.

Machine gun: Rapid-firing weapon used on tanks against attacking aircraft, nonarmored vehicles, enemy strong points, and enemy personnel.

Main Battle Tank (MBT): Heavily gunned, heavily armored, and fast tank able to create and exploit its own breakthroughs and fight enemy tanks effectively. Evolved from and has replaced the medium and heavy tank classes.

Mantlet: Armor surrounding the barrel of the main gun where it protrudes through the turret wall.

Medium tank: Now obsolete class of fast tanks with heavy guns but relatively light armor. They were designed to exploit the breakthroughs made by artillery and heavy tanks.

Multipurpose (MP) ammunition: Tank round that can be used for antitank or antipersonnel purposes.

Muzzle: The open end of a gun where the round discharges.

Muzzle brake: A device on a tank's main gun that retards the "kick," or jump, at the muzzle when hot gases and the projectile leave the barrel. The muzzle brake is a tubular device that is screwed or pinned to the end of the barrel. Baffles or vanes inside the tube serve to deflect the gases laterally or backward so that they push the muzzle down or back. The action of the muzzle brake eases the load on the gun's carriage and mounting.

NATO: North Atlantic Treaty Organization, a military alliance of Western European powers with the United States.

Nuclear-biological-chemical (NBC): Refers to warfare using nuclear, biological, or chemical weapons, or to protection against such weapons.

Obstacle/grade performance: Measure of the height of an obstacle a tank can traverse.

Penetrator rods: Solid metal rods mounted inside a sabot or a conventional warhead. Penetrator rods are made of high-strength alloys or of very strong substances, such as titanium or depleted uranium.

Pillbox: A small concrete hut used as protection from tanks and to house antitank weapons.

Pintle: Pin, bolt, or hook to which a gun is attached, giving the gun the ability to turn.

Plate armor: Thin, flat, shaped pieces of steel or other metal.

Pounder: British measure of the size of a gun, relating to the weight of the shell it fires. Thus, a six-pounder gun is usually taken as a 57 millimeter diameter gun.

Power-to-weight ratio: Engine horsepower delivered per pound of tank.

Primer: Ammunition device that ignites the explosive charge of a round.

Pz.Kpfw: Abbreviation for panzerkampfwagen, the German name for their World War II tanks.

Ranging machine gun: Usually a .50 caliber or larger machine gun mounted coaxially with the main gun. One or more tracer rounds are fired from the machine gun. Their impact is measured through a gun sight and the resulting information is used to aim the main gun. Ranging machine guns have largely been replaced by laser range finders.

Reactive armor: Armor that explodes when struck by an attacking round, defusing the impact of the round. Especially effective against HEAT rounds.

Recoil: Main gun's kickback after firing; a turret must be large enough to accommodate a gun's recoil.

Reconnaissance vehicle: Fast, lightly armored, and usually lightly gunned vehicle that probes enemy lines to gain an appreciation of the enemy's strength and disposition.

Retrofit: To re-equip a tank with new parts, as a larger gun, that were not available when the tank was manufactured.

Return roller wheels: Guide wheels or rollers often found above the road wheels that assist in guiding the tank track during its revolutions.

Rifled gun: Gun whose barrel has **lands** (see entry). Compare **Smoothbore gun**.

Road wheels: Wheels on either side of the tank under which the caterpillar tread passes. The road wheels guide the tread during its revolutions and help to absorb shock.

Sabot: Metal or plastic jacket surrounding a warhead. It prevents the escape of gases ahead of the warhead, allowing a larger-bore gun to be used.

Self-propelled weapon: Gun or howitzer, often built on a tank chassis and hull, that moves itself, needing no towing.

Semicombustible cartridge: Shell that burns up, except for the base and primer, after firing. This makes reloading easier and eliminates empty shells in the tank.

Smoke discharger: A device to conceal a tank through the production of smoke. There are two types. The mortar type is usually mounted on the hull or turret of a tank and fires mortar shells that discharge large volumes of smoke. The second type feeds heavy oil into the manifold of a tank engine to create large volumes of smoke.

Smoothbore gun: Gun barrel without **lands** (see entry). These barrels provide less friction and therefore more power to a shot. Often, smoothbore guns use **fin-stabilized rounds**. Compare **Rifled gun**.

Snorkel: Breathing tube that allows an air-breathing engine to operate under water.

Spall: Scrapes or pieces of metal knocked off one side of armor by impact on the opposite side.

Spall liner: Sheet of kevlar, aluminum, or other material applied to the inside wall of an armored vehicle to trap spalled metal.

Sponson: Structure or platform that projects from the side of a tank and holds a gun.

Sprocket wheels: See **Drive wheels**.

Stabaloy: A steel alloy used on modern tanks. The exact composition is classified.

Tank destroyer: A concept in armored warfare that is rapidly becoming obsolete but used widely toward the end of World War II. The tank destroyer is a conventional tank—usually light or medium class—that is lightly armored but heavily gunned. Its function is to seek out and destroy enemy tanks. Its survival depends on the accuracy and range of its main gun as well as its speed and agility.

Tracer: Material used in artillery, tank guns, and small arms. A trail of smoke is left to show the gunner how close the round traveled toward the target.

Thermal imager: Instrument that presents a picture in the infrared radiation band.

Thermal sight: Infrared detector for use by gunners that presents an image of the target with range coordinates.

Thermal heat sleeve: Anti-infrared radiation covering for an armored vehicle's main gun.

Turret: Movable assembly on top of an armored vehicle's hull that holds the main gun. The turret may also contain crewmembers and ancillary machine guns.

Up-armor: To retrofit a tank with thicker armor.

Up-gun: To retrofit a tank with a more powerful main gun.

Warsaw Pact: Military alliance of Eastern European communist countries with the Soviet Union.